ADVANCE PRAISE FOR *When Kids Fly*

Sally Fryer Dietz is one of the nation's leading experts in the treatment of children with developmental delays and learning differences, helping them grow up to be happy and productive adults. In her new book, *When Kids Fly*, she reasons that children's brains and bodies must develop in concert, and that no child should ever be presumed to have limitations. It's a book full of heart, conviction, and joy, and it offers tremendous advice and hope to parents determined to give their own children every advantage as they grow.

John Matthew Upledger, CEO
Upledger Institute International
International Alliance of Healthcare Educators

Early in her long career, Sally Fryer Dietz vowed to make profound differences in the lives of children with sensory motor development issues. *When Kids Fly* is a guidebook for parents eager to give their children every advantage as they grow up, one that will also greatly benefit teachers and medical professionals dedicated to bringing the best to the children in their care. It's also a moving and spirit-lifting account of how Sally Fryer Dietz's own dedication to her work has dramatically bettered the lives of thousands of children, including her own son. A must-have book for all parents who want their children to fly!

Kenneth E. Salyer, M.D., FACS, FAAP, CMSA (hon.)
Founder and Chairman, World Craniofacial Foundation
Author of *A Life That Matters*

When Kids Fly is a breakthrough book that will change the lives of thousands of children who currently struggle with developmental delays and learning differences. Read it and share it with other parents, teachers, and medical caregivers. It's a book that proves that every child can grow up successfully with the right kind of help and encouragement, regardless of the initial obstacles she faces. Sally Fryer Dietz is a nationally renowned developmental specialist who has made it her life's work to help children grow into happy and productive adults. This is an enormously important new book!

Judy Kyle, Ph.D.
Family Counselor, Dallas Texas

WHEN KIDS FLY!

WHEN KIDS FLY!

Solutions for Children with
Sensory Integration Challenges

SALLY FRYER DIETZ, PT, CST-D

Bascom Hill Publishing Group
Minneapolis, MN

BASCOM HILL
PUBLISHING GROUP

Bascom Hill Publishing Group
322 First Avenue N, 5th floor
Minneapolis, MN 55401
612.455.2294
www.bascomhillpublishing.com

ISBN-13: 978-1-63413-609-9
LCCN: 2015909993

Distributed by Itasca Books

Cover design by Ilona Ratajczak, Ilona DESIGN
Cover photograph by Nino Pinelli
Typeset by Sophie Chi
Edited for Bascom Hill by Robert Christian Schmidt

The names of all the children in this book have been changed (except those of the author's two sons, Alex and Max).
Author Websites: www.whenkidsfly.com & www.iptkids.com

Printed in the United States of America

In loving memory of my dad,
who made sure to let me know he always believed in me.

Every child has an inner timetable for growth—
a pattern unique to him. . . .
Growth is not steady, forward, upward progression.
It is instead a switchback trail; three steps forward,
two back, one around the bushes,
and a few simply standing, before another forward leap.

Dorothy Corkille Briggs

There is always one moment in childhood when the door
opens and lets the future in.

Graham Greene

Contents

An Introduction

------◆------

Alex

Alex, my firstborn, was born in San Francisco on June 14, 1988, and was blessedly perfect in every way—but what is perfect? He had ten fingers and ten toes; he would sleep in my arms, coo contentedly, and even smile in his sleep. His first year seemed to pass smoothly enough, considering that he didn't come with a manual, and we learned about each other together.

I'll never forget the time I was pushing him in a grocery cart while we shopped. A curious and active child, his arms seemed to have the amazing ability to extend from his seat in the cart out to the items on the shelves. To help keep him entertained and out of trouble, I had given him a nice cold block of Monterey Jack cheese to teethe on, not expecting his two little front teeth to actually break through the packaging. But, by the time we got home, he was struggling to breathe due to a sudden asthma attack triggered by an allergy to milk that I hadn't known about until that moment.

I rushed him to his pediatrician's office, where he received his first shot of epinephrine. He was fine, but it was obvious that his sensitivity to milk products would mean making sure in the future that nothing he consumed contained any of the milk proteins that had set him off in the first place. Despite numerous allergy tests over the following years, we never really knew the exact cause of his persistent runny nose or the tickle that contributed to an annoying clearing of his throat, both of which we knew were potential signs of an allergic irritation. And there were the nights, too, when nothing seemed to settle him down despite him having a clean diaper, full tummy, and constant cradling in my arms as we rocked in our favorite glider chair. It was more exhausting than upsetting, and I grew to enjoy our long middle of the night rocks together. This was what motherhood was all about, right?

By the time we moved to Dallas, when he was two and a half, Alex was a mobile, active, and happy little guy. For some reason, the "terrible twos" seemed to elude him, yet when he hit three, this all seemed to change. The word "no" was a constant for both of us and his activity level reached new heights. Although we had planned to have a larger family, I decided to put off having another baby, unable to imagine how I was going to handle caring for two children at the same time, especially if they were all this energetic. It took me another two years, and my thirty-fifth birthday, before—feeling I really shouldn't put off waiting too much longer—I became pregnant with Max. It's amazing how two children from the same biological parents can be so different and yet so perfect in their own unique ways. It wasn't until I had Max, though, that I realized that some children could actually be a little *easier* to raise than others.

At age three, Alex met his first, and to this day "best," friend. Thriving on each other's energy and impulsivity, he and Luke kept their mothers on constant vigilance. They simply couldn't get enough of each other, and if mischief could be found, they would find it. One day, for example, while playing "super heroes" in their home-made costumes, they used their stick swords to knock off every new, little rose they could find in the garden—certain that the beautiful flowers clearly posed a grave menace to society.

Well before Alex started preschool, it was clear that he was a bright child. He loved books, and frequently gravitated to his favorites, making it appear as if he might turn out to be an early reader. *National Geographic* fish books were among his favorites, and by three-and-a-half he knew most of the fish they featured by their scientific names.

With the societal pressure of putting children in school at younger and younger ages, age three seemed like the ideal time to begin Alex's early education at a nearby Montessori school. He made friends easily, but his favorite remained his dear friend Luke from across the street who, as luck would have it, was also in the same class. At school, Alex repetitively sought out his favorite activities, which allowed him to stay within his comfort zone, avoiding other undertakings that he found more challenging or less "fun." Even so, Alex's desire to learn about the world kept his teachers and me on our toes—like the time he stuck a nut up his nose simply to see how far it would go, resulting in another emergency visit to the pediatrician for a medical extraction.

Other kids liked him, but he was often indifferent toward them, preferring to play with his sole best friend. Always proficient at language, he clearly explained to me one day that he "thought it best to get to know someone for at least a year or two" before he invited them over to play. Because he was recognized as a bright and sensitive child by virtually everyone who encountered him, neither his teachers nor I were concerned—at least in the beginning—that he wasn't interested in the least in handwriting, drawing, or math. He gravitated to natural sciences and building elaborate block structures, avoiding like the plague anything having to do with writing or counting.

I had degrees in both physical therapy and child development, and loved the fact that Alex was a smart, sensitive, and stimulation-seeking child. Coming from a medical family, our premature bias was that he seemed well suited for an eventual career involving medicine, nature, or science. When it came to reading and handwriting, I presumed he just needed a little more time to settle down.

His Montessori-trained teachers were happy to let him do his own thing for a while, too. Yet, when they began to work hard with him on his reading, writing, and math skills at age five, he continued to balk. He was a master avoider, wanting little to do with any of it. He wrote very poorly when he wrote at all and preferred to look at the same books over and over—especially choosing the ones that we had read together over the years. I was actually under the impression that he could read the books he was familiar with at home, until I eventually realized that he had been memorizing the words in these books, rather than actually "reading" them.

(Since that time, I have met many other children who do the same thing: avoiding the visual scanning and processing of individual letters, sounds, and words required for reading fluently. Instead, they memorize easily what they have seen before or heard, repeating back from memory what they remember, and not what they are seeing and processing before them. They tend to see a word as an individual picture, not as a string of symbols representing various ideas or concepts. This can make reading comprehension more of a challenge for these kids, especially as they get older and have more content to absorb and process. As a result, these kids tend to resist reading, or gravitate toward reading the same stories over and over.)

Alex had become so good at this that I wouldn't have known that he had memorized an eye chart in order to avoid wearing glasses, if he hadn't told me himself years later. Even so, when his teacher expressed her concerns and suggested that I have him evaluated for possible learning differences, I was a little taken aback.

This is Alex, I thought—my wonderful, bright, capable, yet somewhat oppositional and willful little boy. Yes, he was certainly "active." Yes, I had to keep my eye on him at all times because he was so often impulsive. Yes, I could now see that reading, writing, and math were not actually his favorite activities, but surely nothing was really *wrong.* After all, he was only five!

Despite my certainty that he was fine, I took Alex to see his pediatrician, as his teachers had suggested. I described the issues his teachers had noticed at school and the physician quickly recommended that we try him on Ritalin. There was no evaluation, only little examination, and no other recommendation made other than the trial use of pharmaceuticals.

As a parent, I can share with you the insecurity that can creep into your parenting skills when your doctor suggests that you do something, especially when you fear that your child may be in trouble and you want to make sure you are doing the right thing. Coming from a medical family, and being married to a doctor, I felt we had no other choice than to take the pediatrician's suggestion and try the medicine. But Alex calmed down *so* much with the Ritalin, that even though he appeared to now be over focused on the things that had previously seemed to bore him, he hardly talked, and moved through his day in slow, almost "automatic" motion. He wasn't rambunctious or animated anymore, and he rarely smiled. When the medication wore off, he became explosive and agitated and was unable to sleep at night, complicating things even further. Soon, he began to show signs of depression and we had no choice but to seek out another opinion about what else we could do to help him.

The developmental pediatrician we saw next suggested we try a different set of medications—a slower-acting stimulant in combination with an antidepressant to help him sleep. When I asked about some other options, like any therapeutic services that might be available, he referred me to a handwriting specialist. Intuitively, I knew there was more to what was going on with Alex than just "handwriting" but at least it seemed to be another option besides medication.

The occupational therapist Alex saw at that point set out to "fix" his writing challenges, but as I might have predicted, that didn't work out well either. As I already knew from my previous work experience as a pediatric therapist in California, when underlying sensory motor issues are getting in the way of a child's development, you can practice writing all day long, but the results are still likely to be minimal (handwriting is often just a symptom of a bigger problem). So, at a friend's suggestion, we were off to specialist number three for educational testing, which we hoped would offer the insight and answers we so desperately wanted—ideally leading us to the help we now knew Alex needed.

The educational diagnostician we went to was one of the most gifted evaluators in Dallas at the time. She performed a comprehensive battery of intellectual and educational performance tests that lasted over several days. Afterwards, we came back for a sit-down meeting to discuss her findings. She reported to me that my son was a boy with very high intelligence, but his writing skills were far below average. The big discrepancy between the two, she said, likely meant that Alex suffered from "dysgraphia," or writing disability, and likely an attention-deficit disorder. She suggested pulling Alex out of the Montessori environment he loved so much and enrolling him in a public school, where he wouldn't stand out as much.

This didn't feel right to me either, and his teachers remained committed to helping Alex succeed. So, instead, I decided to keep him right where he was in his existing Montessori school. I felt that the nurturing environment, where his teachers already knew his strengths and weaknesses—and were still willing to work with us—was a better fit for all of us. I was concerned that moving him into a larger, unfamiliar classroom where he wouldn't stand out was a setup for being lost in the crowd, and not a place where he was going to get any extra attention if he needed it. Not only that, I wanted to be more personally involved as well. I knew in my gut that helping Alex was going to take more than just a shift in the environment or another new medication.

Several more consultations with professionals all yielded similar conclusions: he was a "smart boy," but he had "trouble paying attention."

No one was able to offer real solutions to help him have greater success in learning—or how to find his joy again—and I found myself becoming increasingly frustrated and worried about my child.

Because of my own professional background in pediatrics, learning, and development, I understood that handwriting difficulties and other potential learning differences could not be ignored. But I wasn't having much luck finding a program in Dallas that was set up to address *both* his dysgraphia *and* his overall health and happiness. The mom in me wanted to say, "Hey, he's perfect. He's a *boy*! He's just like his dad." But, as a professional, I understood that I had to do something. The combination of the increasing handwriting issues, the impulsivity, and the snowballing frustration and depression he was exhibiting *did* call—loudly—for therapeutic attention.

So, I stopped listening to everyone else and began to search metropolitan Dallas for what I knew from experience would work: a sensory-motor development clinic where Alex could get the kind of help I believed he needed—only to discover that it didn't exist. I knew exactly where I would have taken him if I had still lived in San Francisco: back to the Learning and Development Center, where I once had been part of a physical and occupational therapy program focused on utilizing sensory integration techniques to get to the root of, and effectively treat, learning and developmental problems. Sensory integration therapy is a treatment technique that has been utilized by therapists since the 50s when occupational therapist and developmental psychologist Jean Ayres, PhD, OTR, brought focus to what many currently refer to as "sensory integration dysfunction." Treatment focuses on techniques to enhance learning, attention, behavior, and motor development. Unfortunately, even after looking extensively, I simply couldn't find anything like that in Dallas back in 1994. I had only a single option, it seemed, and that was to create a clinic myself—one that would make use of a wide range of multidisciplinary, patient-tailored therapies that I knew would work. A clinic that would help children grow into healthy, happy, productive adults, and one where prescription drugs would *not* be the only option.

My goal was to create a place where I would want to take my own child and really "get what I was paying for." I wanted a fabulous, inviting environment with great specialists who possessed a repertoire of proven therapeutic interventions that really worked. The clinic would offer treatments that would make a difference in families' lives without insurance companies dictating what each unique child needed. As a therapist who had worked in early intervention before, I knew what worked and what didn't. I wasn't going to waste anyone's time or money, and I wanted to make a difference for children like Alex—and for families like mine.

A good friend of mine who was a licensed professional counselor shared with me how challenging it was for families to drive all over town to acquire services for their children. I also knew it never worked for a parent to be her child's therapist (regardless of the level of the parent's training), and that developmental issues were rarely related to only one system. This led to a group of us coming together in 1994 to form a professional pediatric therapy association which included physical, occupational, and speech therapy, as well as counseling services and social skills practice. Soon, Alex was spending several days a week in our multifaceted gym with several of the therapists, and his life began to change.

Fortunately, his school was right around the corner from the clinic—which was part of the reason I picked the location where the clinic remains today. I would pick him up from school a little before noon several days a week and bring him to the clinic, where he would work with one of my associates—swinging through hanging obstacle courses, flying like Superman, and throwing bean bags at targets for fifty minutes before going back to join his teachers and classmates.

He would light up and engage in the gym—and before long not even handwriting was a burden to him. The changes in him were incredible, and soon he no longer needed to be on medication. His teachers, his father, and I all agreed that Alex was doing great and was thriving once again. It felt great to have my son back, full of smiles and natural curiosity.

Then and Now

When I was a child, I'm certain that I, too, had some underlying sensory integration challenges—the reality is, we *all* do! It's simply a matter of how many challenges a person must face that ultimately determines success or failure. The difference between Alex's situation and mine was that I grew up in the 1950s and 1960s in an idyllic community in the Bay Area of California where we had enormous freedom to play, explore, and grow.

We lived in a safe little city called Piedmont, in the hills above Berkeley and Oakland. We walked to school every day, rode our bikes, and ran around our neighborhood doing exactly as we pleased—playing ball with neighbor kids, building tunnels through our mother's hedges, and creating elaborate "forts" from cardboard boxes. We climbed high into the big cherry tree in the backyard, where sheets we had "borrowed" from the linen closet served as hammocks that wrapped around us like cocoons. We would tuck ourselves inside a wash barrel and push each other down the driveway onto the lawn below, as well as run through the sprinklers and zoom down a "slip and slide" on the grass hill in our yard, landing in a big mud puddle at the bottom. Our arms and legs were constantly coated with mud and grass stains, but they were nothing a scrub in the bath couldn't remove.

Summers were spent at Lake Tahoe, where our dad pulled us through the water while he ran knee deep, pulling a plank of boards behind him, which we called our "aquaplane." While primarily a ton of fun, the activity helped to develop our balance, while he got his work out. Falls into the cold lake woke up our nervous systems and reaction times as we scrambled to get up out of the water almost as soon as we hit it. We canoed, sailed, and hiked, all physical activities involving nature and the building of strength, coordination, and skill. In the evenings, we came together as a family enjoying plenty of music, songs, and skits, enriching our creative spirits. A hammock between two large pine trees became my favorite place to relax and dream, with no other distractions around aside from the sounds of nature. Yes, those were the "good old days" before parents had to worry about kidnappings, too much electronic media, and whether one of us wasn't reading or writing before the age of five.

I was a shy kid in those early years, and I suspect I was also a bit "low tone," a symptom caused by extra-flexible joints and tendons, causing the muscles to have to work harder to do even the simplest things like sitting still in a chair or standing up straight. Young children with low tone can often be observed sitting in what is called a "W position" with their feet splayed out behind their hips, a passive way of supporting the body upright by resting on the joints, rather than using postural support. Like many other children, including Alex, I had a hard time sitting still in my chair and was constantly reminded to "stand up straight!" I was also terrible at handwriting, but the only option for help back then was to be forced into writing letters over and over in a specially lined handwriting booklet—a task I absolutely hated. It is no wonder that I didn't like school in those days. I had to write so slowly in order to write "correctly" that I missed many of the other details needed to complete the assignments correctly and efficiently. It is actually easier to move quickly than it is to move slowly, so if all of your attention goes toward one particular task like writing, what happens to the other directions? A great way to compensate is to write as little as possible, which contributes to a condition called "poor written expression," something Alex and I both shared. Copying things off the blackboard in the front of the room was even more challenging, and my schoolwork suffered.

I survived my early education with the help of tutors, tennis, piano, and skiing—all of which I loved, my tutors and skiing in particular. Speeding down the slopes of the Sierras gave me freedom, a great way work on my coordination, and the adrenalin rush I needed to feel alive. My tutors helped me feel special and offered me the one-on-one attention that helped me make sense of what I was trying to learn, because too many distractions in the classroom made it hard to pay attention. With those tools in place, learning became fun again—and I could finally feel good about myself.

In the big picture, I was one of the lucky ones. I graduated from high school a year early, went off to college, and chose child development as my major—primarily because it was something I thought my own life to that point had already taught me something about.

Today, by comparison, Alex and millions of other kids are growing up in an entirely different world. Even in small towns, parents would be considered irresponsible or plain crazy if they simply turned their children loose to play wherever and however they liked. Lawns, parks, forests, and meadows are foreign lands for many thousands of kids, and shopping malls are today's equivalents of the safe and quiet neighborhoods where we used to play. Babies spend most of their time in car seats or "bouncers," while their older siblings entertain themselves with video games and electronic tablets instead of bikes, balls, bats, and tire swings.

Digital technology has dramatically altered all of our lives, and it has radically changed the ways in which children develop. Movies on demand, text messages, and Google Maps are wonderful tools, of course. Yet, I believe we can't ignore technology's downside— especially when it comes to the developing brain of a child and the behavioral problems we create from a world comprised almost entirely of highly visual stimulation, limited sensory motor experiences, and an expectation of instant gratification for both child and parent.

We've understood for a long time that play is an absolutely essential component of each young person's developing life. It's through play that children develop their skeletal and muscular systems, their sensory systems, their visual perceptual skills, and (ultimately) their language and cognition skills. Physical play is as vital for each child's development as good nutrition, but increasingly children's "play" is limited to couches and living room floors, with detrimental consequences for their health—physical, emotional, and educational.

No doubt there are many factors that are responsible for the sharp rise in developmental disorders, however many professionals involved in early education and child development are convinced that the way technology promotes sedentary play also has a significant role. The American Academy of Pediatrics has even come out with a recommendation that children under the age of two not be exposed to *any* technology at all. With that in mind, let me share some statistics with you.

In 2013, it was reported by the American Psychiatric Association that 5% of children in the United States have ADHD (American Psychiatric Association. *Diagnostic and Statistical Manual of Mental Disorders*, Fifth edition: DSM-5. Washington: American Psychiatric Association, 2013.) However, in practice, it appears as though the number of children actually being diagnosed with ADHD is much higher.

It is well known in clinical circles that individuals with symptoms of ADHD are much more likely to have social skills problems, major injuries, hospitalizations, and emergency room admissions than those without a history of ADHD. In adolescence and adulthood, the risks of alcohol and drug addictions go up, as well as the incidence of motor vehicle accidents and unemployment.

In the U.S., the number of individuals with developmental and learning disabilities has risen significantly since the late 1990s—a trend driven mostly by surges in the diagnosis of autism and ADHD. In addition, many of these children end up leaving school or avoid higher education because they can't get the help they need.

Perhaps most unsettling of all developmental statistics is the rise in autism. In 2014, the Centers for Disease Control and Prevention (CDC) reported that 1 in 68 children were currently being identified with Autism Spectrum Disorder. Autism is a reflection of severe sensory processing challenges in an individual. It is often referred to as a "spectrum disorder" because of the wide range of possible sensory motor symptoms, skills, and levels of impairment—including social discomfort, communication difficulties, and repetitive and stereotyped behaviors. Along that same spectrum, some children may only be mildly impaired, while others are severely disabled. Currently, an estimated 1.5 million Americans have some form of autism, and the number rises every year. In fact, the U.S. Department of Education reports that autism is growing at a rate between ten and seventeen percent each year. At this rate, the number of Americans with some form of autism may reach four million in the next decade. Autism knows no racial, ethnic, or social boundaries, and pays no attention to family income, lifestyle, or educational levels. It can affect any family, and any child. And although the overall incidence of autism is consistent around the globe, it is four times more prevalent in boys than in girls, for reasons scientists do not yet understand.

Since 1994, we have seen a significant increase in the demand for therapeutic services, in part due to the wide range of developmental challenges that can be helped by sensory integration therapy. In fact, autistic children share many of the same kinds of challenges as children who have been diagnosed with ADHD and other sensory processing disorders. While assigning a name or a diagnosis to a collection of symptoms a child is expressing can be helpful in treatment (and to insurance companies as they determine benefits), many parents find identifying a child by her diagnoses to be alarming. It's important to remember that we never treat a diagnosis; we treat a child. *Every child is unique*, whether he is minimally challenged, severely handicapped, or— like the vast majority of the children we see—somewhere in between. A diagnosis is just a name, and it's important not to run from it or hide behind it. Ideally, it can help others first to understand the challenges your child is having, and then to be of help. Teachers, for example, are more likely to go out of their way to assist a child in finding greater success in the classroom when her diagnosis gives them a clear sense of what she is facing.

As you consider your own strengths and weaknesses when it comes to sight, hearing, motor control, language, and cognition, it's easy to realize that we all exist somewhere along a sensory integration spectrum. Terms like "normal" or "typical" simply refer to the mid-range, not to an absolute. It is better, I'm convinced, to consider that each of our children approach the world each in their own unique ways, just as my son did. Some of these children simply need a little help along the way, and what could be more *normal* than that?

When Kids Fly

Alex ultimately thrived, and this book is the direct result of my experiences both as a mother of a child with sensory-processing issues and as the founder and twenty-year director of Integrative Pediatric Therapy (IPT). At this stage in my thirty-plus-year career, we've been blessed to have helped thousands of children live healthier, more productive lives.

When Kids Fly is a book for worried parents like I once was— parents who want the very best for their children—for teachers who understand that some children have needs that simply cannot be met in the classroom, and for medical professionals who are committed to multi-disciplinary approaches for the treatment of sensory motor development issues. It's a book that promises help. I've never seen even the most severely impaired child whose life couldn't be made richer and more satisfying with the right kind of therapy, and the large majority of children with sensory integration problems grow up to become happy and productive adolescents and adults.

In the break room of our Hillcrest Road clinic in Dallas, a small pink pig with wings on his back is suspended by fishing line above the table where busy therapists eat a quick lunch before getting back to their patients. He's whimsical, this pig who can fly, but he's there for a reason, too: to remind each of us that when we all work together and really listen to the needs of a child, we can accomplish just about anything, enrich a child's life, and set him up for great success. Children with problems that have vexed their parents and teachers for months and sometimes years can find real help without feeling worthless and defeated. They can be transformed with the right kind of intervention and teamwork—enriched with new skill sets, beaming with pride. When kids are released from the obstacles that hold them down and are allowed to "fly" in a metaphorical sense, they are able to gain the freedom and security to accomplish virtually anything they set out to do. In other words, I believe there really are no limits, aside from the ones you put on someone, so why not help our kids to "head for the sky" and really "fly"?

CHAPTER 1

————•————

When something's not quite right with your child . . .
Or, when to worry

A majority of the children who receive the benefits of therapy are beautiful, smart, rapidly growing, school-age kids—more than a little reminiscent of Alex—about whom something seems *not quite right*, but it's hard to put a finger on what that "something" is. It is common for parents to have only just become aware of their child's challenges when teachers inform them of an academic weakness or behavior that deserves attention.

Because parents live in such close proximity to their children and observe their development in small, daily increments—and because one of a parent's most important jobs is simply to love her children *as they are*—it is often extremely difficult to see (and subsequently acknowledge) when a child might be having a problem beyond his control, one that can be corrected when identified early enough. That's something I have personally experienced both as a therapist *and* a parent.

If an eighteen month old still isn't crawling or stiffens and resists when he is cuddled, those are early signs that might raise concerns to some. But, for a first-time parent trying to do the best for his child, how can he tell, at three, how clumsy is too clumsy? When is being a picky eater a problem? At six, how messy does handwriting have to be before it's considered a red flag? Is a child simply shy or is she encountering problems in interacting with others? Is she a "bundle of energy" or is she hyper-active? And how many of our kids are "just like us," a "chip off the old block," or simply "unique"?

Answers to these questions are always child specific—every one of us develops in our own unique pattern and at our own pace. Yet there are a number of classical signals that parents, teachers, and medical professionals can—and should—be aware of. As a rule of thumb, one or two red flags may not be cause for major concern, but several in combination may well be a sign that something is not quite right and early intervention could help.

As a child enters preschool or kindergarten, for example, he may have difficulty following instructions, or he may over-focus on one activity while being reluctant to shift to a new one. Or maybe he's always pushing into his friend's space, over-touching, or playing roughly with materials and other kids. Perhaps she's a young girl who breaks her pencils frequently because she writes with such heavy pressure, or a boy who just *can't* sit still, even for a moment.

In general, if a teacher suggests to parents that their child may have a problem, that suggestion deserves attention. Teachers have the advantage of observing a wide range of children in their classes. Even if they can't identify what the exact problem is, they often know when a child is having more trouble than her peers. "Normal," "typical," and "average" all encompass a wide spectrum of development. A smart child who does not appear to be living up to his potential can signal trouble that can often be helped by therapy. From my own experience, I knew very well that five-year-old Alex could be a challenge and that he didn't like to color, but it wasn't until his teachers brought their concerns about how he was struggling with writing and wasn't following directions to my attention that, in concert, these behaviors began to point to his need for therapy.

It is important for you to know what the red flags are, not so that you frighten yourself about what your child's potential weaknesses might be, but so that you will have help in identifying the very things that truly *can* be helped by therapy when identified early. Even if your child demonstrates half a dozen of these issues, that does *not* mean she won't grow up to be an absolutely normal, capable, and wonderful adult. Even when the mountain of challenges seems to be insurmountable, the right interventions at the right times can make all the difference in a happy, successful outcome. Even children with big hills to climb have the potential to make incredible successes and are far ahead of where they would have been without help.

Developmental "Red Flags"

All of us—from the most severely challenged to the individuals who appear to do everything with great ease—live on the same developmental spectrum. Children grow and develop on significantly different schedules and at different paces and, therefore, acquire appropriate developmental milestones at widely ranging times. Girls often reach these milestones sooner than boys, but not always, and growing boys can appear "wilder" and more full of energy than their female peers, but that is also not an absolute.

If you recognize one of the red flags I outline below—or even several of them—it does *not* mean your child—and you—are necessarily in for hard times. Red flags signal nothing more than the likelihood that a formal evaluation of your child's development may be a good idea. This is especially true if you consider that an evaluation could lead to therapy, if indeed it's needed, and a great outcome.

During your baby's *first year of life*, you should seek advice from a medical professional if you notice:

- Your baby is doing too much arching of his back. This can

be a sign of increased tightness in the muscles of the back (a postural muscle imbalance), colic (stomach discomfort contributing to a crying, fussy baby), or reflux (abnormal spitting up of stomach contents after eating).

- He seems to resist being on his stomach.
- Your baby seems weak and floppy with a persistent head lag (this can be a sign of a neurological problem, or developmental delay).
- Your baby preferentially uses one arm over the other or always seems to be looking to the same side (this can be a sign of a neurological problem or musculo-skeletal imbalance).
- Your baby cannot follow your gaze or has poor eye contact (this may signal developmental delay, neurologic disorder, or visual weakness).
- Your baby has an irregularly shaped head or head flattening (which could indicate possible structural or muscular conditions).
- Your baby rarely babbles, or seems to have slow language or vocalizations emerging (may indicate a hearing loss or other neurological problem).
- Your baby has trouble feeding. This can be caused by structural problems in the mouth or an oral motor muscle imbalance. In addition, tactile sensitivity can play a part in frequent gagging or trouble swallowing.
- He smiles or laughs only infrequently, or not at all (signaling a lag in social interaction or communication delay).

As he grows and develops, moving towards *becoming a toddler*, you should also notice if he:

- Doesn't appear to recognize faces (affecting socialization).
- Has problems rolling over, crawling, sitting, standing, or walking (interfering with age-appropriate motor development).

- Excessively drools or "mouths" objects (may signal muscle weakness in the mouth or a need to seek comfort through the mouth).
- Keeps his hands clenched in fists at all times (may indicate a neurologic problem).
- Startles easily (represents a sensitive nervous system).
- Has a hard time settling down, frequently appearing uncomfortable, fussy, and crying.
- Resists being held or dislikes being cuddled (may be exhibiting early signs of tactile defensiveness, caused by an over-sensitivity to touch).
- Seems to be losing his skills after they have been acquired (may be a sign of a significant developmental or neurological disorder).

Kids make dramatic developmental strides *between ages three and five*. It's a time when motor and language skills blossom, and personalities flourish. During this time, pay attention if your child:

- Holds his hands over his ears in response to loud noises (a sign of auditory or tactile sensitivity).
- Is a picky eater (a sign of muscle imbalance in the mouth or sensitivity to touch or smells affecting eating).
- Stuffs (or "pockets") food in his cheeks (a sign of a mis-perception of touch, interfering with the normal movement of food in the mouth that is needed to swallow effectively).
- Is sensitive to textures on the skin, resisting tags in shirts, sock seams, and anything that may be perceived as being a "scratchy" fabric (a sign of tactile defensiveness).
- Fights baths, or is sensitive to having his hair washed (a sign of tactile defensiveness or trouble with the ears and/or vestibular system when the head is tilted backwards).
- Is a poor sleeper, has trouble getting to sleep and staying asleep.

Good sleep is critical for adequate attention in school. Sleep deprivation can be a cause of inattention and restlessness during the day.

- Snores while sleeping, a potential sign of enlarged tonsils or adenoids associated with sleep apnea and poor sleep, leading to inattention and behavioral concerns.
- Shows little interest in playing with others (social delays).
- Avoids playground activities (sensory sensitivity, social and motor delays).
- Frequently bumps into people or objects (poor body awareness).
- Trips or falls often (poor body awareness, balance and coordination challenges).
- Has a hard time sitting still in a chair, props his body into awkward positions, or appears restless when unsupported (can be a sign of muscle weakness and poor postural stability, contributing to inattention and decreased fine-motor skills like handwriting).
- Is fearful on slides and high swings, or is scared when his feet are off the ground or his head is tipped backwards (vestibular deficits causing fear reactions and poor body awareness).
- Walks or runs on tiptoes (may be caused by sensitivity to touch through the bottoms of the feet).
- Jumps in place, flaps his hands, or rocks his body (helps to soothe or activate the nervous system. Frequently associated with signs of anxiety).
- Moves excessively—or seems to avoid movement (a sign of postural weakness, vestibular and proprioceptive deficits. It is easier to move than to stand or sit still).
- Overreacts in response to touch, tastes, sounds, or odors.
- Has difficulty transitioning from one activity to another

(related to inefficient sensory processing from the environment).

- Has real difficulty using scissors, doing puzzles, or coloring inside lines (appears as delayed fine-motor skills in school).
- Breaks toys or crayons easily (poor body awareness and proprioceptive deficits).

By *first grade, or around age six,* we should have a capable child on our hands. He should be able to engage in long, detailed conversations, talking about the past, present, future, and imaginary events. He can cut out simple shapes, color within the lines, and entertain himself. His pronunciation of letters and words is clear and he enjoys retelling stories and describing events. During this time, his friends become more important, and he can follow two-step directions fairly consistently.

At this stage of development, your child's unique personality and capabilities should become quite obvious, making it increasingly easy to see if something is not quite right. Yet it's easy to be fooled at this point. Kids are smart, and they will gravitate toward the things which they excel at and enjoy doing. Pay attention to the variety—or its absence— in your child's choices and play, and teachers and parents both should make note when a child:

- Finds it hard to follow instructions, especially those with multiple steps.
- Has difficulty paying attention or sitting still.
- Needs more practice than other kids to learn new skills.
- Is overly focused and resistant to shifting to a new task.
- Shows delays in handwriting and other fine-motor skills.
- Breaks toys and pencils frequently.
- Has trouble reproducing shapes or letters.
- Draws with pressure that's too heavy or too light.
- Actively dislikes handwriting or written work.
- Regularly reverses letters like b and d.

- Has difficulty spacing letters on a line.
- Seems overly clumsy or accident prone.
- Has low muscle tone, slouching or propping himself on furniture.
- Can't sit still at the dinner table.
- Avoids—or seeks out—jumping or high swinging.
- Avoids sports or physical games.
- Seeks out physically aggressive activities, and tends to play rough.
- Overreacts or underreacts to touch, tastes, sounds, or odors.
- Dislikes grooming, such as bathing, brushing his teeth, washing his face, trimming his nails, and getting haircuts.
- Is sensitive to clothing tags, seams, and fabrics.
- Wears the same clothes again and again.
- Is overly active or unable to slow down.
- Finds it hard to make friends, and prefers the company of adults.
- Has poor self-esteem, or lacks self-confidence.

You've probably noticed that many of these behaviors are opposites of each other. It is not uncommon for one child to be overly sensitive to a stimulus and another to be under-responsive to the same thing. You can even see opposite reactions from the same child, varying from day to day, or even hour to hour, depending on how much sleep he got or what he had to eat.

If you feel a worried knot in your stomach after reading these lists of red flags, let me remind you once more that we *all* have challenges in certain areas; it's only when we have a few too many that problems arise. If I had read similar lists twenty years ago, just as Alex first began to attend his Montessori school, his teachers and I would have agreed, that, yes, he had a hard time paying attention and sitting still; that, yes, instructions could be challenging for him; and, yes, handwriting was not his favorite thing. I would have agreed, too, that quite often he found it almost impossible to really slow down and listen to what I was trying to tell him. When I finally took the time to look more closely, those were many of the same red flags that, thankfully, got him into therapy.

Your Sensational Child

Alex was one of those kids who could have easily slipped through the cracks. He was smart and engaging, but he just wasn't performing at a level that we all believed he was capable of—and, in those days, therapy was reserved for kids who fell *way* below the mean. Of course, medication was an easily available option, but was it the answer? Alex was what the Sensory Processing Disorder Foundation (http://spdfoundation.net) refers to as a "Sensational Kid"—a boy whose young brain didn't process sensory input in the same way that the majority of his peers' brains did, getting in the way of how he put things together in his head and not allowing him to function as well as he potentially could.

When Sensational Kids receive sensory information via sight, smell, hearing, taste, touch, or their vestibular and proprioceptive systems, their brains don't always know what to do with that information. They have a hard time making cognitive sense out of it—in other words, how to "process" it. Their bodies tend to become disorganized and confused, causing them to bounce around the room overreacting to the sensory input they receive from the world around them, or they shut down, sometimes not reacting at all. The signs can be subtle or quite obvious—if you know what to look for. The good thing is, when identified early enough, these kids really can get better.

Sensational Kids can have real difficulty functioning at school, in public, or even at home. They might accidentally bump into others or appear to intentionally disrupt or even hit them. They can be eerily quiet and withdrawn, or have frequent meltdowns and tantrums. It's not uncommon for them to have trouble eating or wearing certain types of clothing—the tag on the inside of a shirt collar can feel unbearable, for example, as if it were a fingernail scratching up and down the back of their neck. Sensational Kids may be wary—or even fearful—of new experiences because they are unsure whether their sensory alarms might go off. Bright lights in supermarkets, the sound of a garage door opening, the movement of a merry-go-round, or even the texture of yogurt or spaghetti can cause a breakdown that seems to come out of nowhere.

These kids sometimes struggle to run or ride a bike. Learning how to tie their shoelaces can seem all but impossible. Some cry and scream frequently; others appear simply to stare off into space. No two kids are ever exactly alike, and Sensational Kids are no exception—there are lots of them everywhere. Scientists say that as many as one in twenty children have at least one or more sensory processing challenges, but teachers likely would tell you that this number is much higher.

If you have begun to suspect *your* child might have some of these challenges, you're already taking a vitally important step simply by trying to understand it. Before you go any further, though, remember that, while developmental delays and sensory processing issues must be paid attention to, they need not make you fear for your child's future. Sensational Kids are, more often than not, extremely intelligent. With early intervention, you can help set any kid up for the success they deserve.

Given the possibility that therapy is in your child's future, do keep in mind that "therapy," itself, is an adult term. It's nothing more than the attempted remediation of a health problem—not something that's inherently strange or mysterious or pejorative. In the world of pediatrics, we tend to refer to therapy sessions as "exercise time" or "gym time." Kids come up with their own terms like my "fun time" or "play time." No matter what you want to call it, we believe that all children are full of potential waiting to be engaged, and these sessions are a great avenue for this to happen. When something is not quite right with a child, it is often the child who suffers, first, by reacting in a way that takes her away from the very activities that can help her the most. Therapy is simply a way to help unlock potential and build body connections so everything can work better and kids really can thrive. No child receives therapy because she is "broken." Instead, think of these kids as "sensational," and simply in need of a new way to approach the world so they can make better sense of it.

The Naysayers

If you look very far into the possibility of seeking sensory integration therapy for your child, you'll almost certainly run into someone who believes that it is simply the latest therapy *du jour*—that it's expensive, that it takes a long time, and that there is little scientific evidence for its efficacy. In this Internet era, it's easy to find criticism of virtually anything, if you look for it—no matter how valuable or life-enhancing it is. And there are certainly people out there who, for whatever reasons, have had negative experiences with these therapies and have critical things to say.

Some criticism comes from the fact that you can't treat each young patient in precisely the same way and get precisely the same results, which is what research utilizing the "scientific method" measures; you can't spin a six-year-old boy clockwise in a frog swing ten times, measure how his eyes move before and after in response to the movement, and demonstrate the same results with *every* six-year-old boy. Sensory integration therapy works because it is an individualized program, geared toward creating gains in each individual child. Everyone is different, so every program must be different as well.

What therapists can prove is that *everyone* does better, although at different rates and levels of improvement. There are many case studies and examples of successes in the professional literature to back this up.

When parents and teachers rave about the wonderful changes they see in a child undergoing sensory integration therapy, that's the *best* kind of proof. For those of us who see its dramatic results virtually every day, we have constant confirmation that the work we do is worthwhile. And, for the parents who get to live with their children and interact with them day and night, sensory integration therapy is a godsend that they tend to affirm they cannot imagine doing without.

I have been personally and professionally involved in sensory integration therapy since the 1970s, and my belief in this work—and the way in which it sets young lives on their best course—grows stronger with each passing year.

CHAPTER 2

———•———

Making sense of your child's senses . . .
And what they have to do with your child's development

Back when I was in grade school, I learned—as you probably did—
that each of us has five senses: sight, smell, hearing, taste, and
touch. These "sensory systems" help us gather information about our
world in fairly obvious ways: we can see the people in front of us; we
can hear the barking of a dog; and we can taste and smell the sweetness
of our favorite cookie. We can even feel the comfort of our mother's
arms or our favorite blanket. But what gives us the information about
how and where our body is moving through space—and how do we
register gravity, movement, and balance? The truth is there are two
more systems that are also critical to your child's sensory motor
development: the *proprioceptive* and *vestibular* systems.

The proprioceptive system allows us to process critical information
through our joints, ligaments, and muscles. Our vestibular system
registers information through the inner ear about where our head is in
relation to objects around us. When these two systems work together,
we can regulate our posture and tone, and stay oriented in space.
When they don't work together (or when they register information
inefficiently), they can cause a child to appear disorganized, or out of
control, as he has trouble filtering and interpreting what's going on
around him. Kids who have trouble processing information through

any of their sensory systems can feel overloaded or out of sorts, or simply find themselves unable to organize themselves in a meaningful way. Imagine having a traffic jam of sorts in your brain; that's the reality for these kids, and it can make growing and developing far more challenging for them than for their peers.

The essence of sensory processing involves three different processes: sensory discrimination (filtering out input), sensory modulation (sorting through the information), and motor planning (putting it all together and, ultimately, developing movement skills).

The first step in sensory processing is taking in and registering sensory information through our central nervous system. Millions of sensory neurons, which are found throughout our body, receive this input from the senses and send it to our brains via our peripheral nervous systems. Some information travels through the spinal cord, while some enters directly through the cranial nerves, like the registration of smell.

When your child experiences a disturbance in receiving sensory input (or, conversely, a flood of information all at once), and his brain is trying its best to interpret it, it can be challenging to get him to listen to you and pay attention. This inability to focus can present itself in a variety of ways, which can be both conflicting and confusing to everyone involved. For example, the interpretation of sound as being too much or too loud from whatever source—anything from a noisy circus show to the honk of a car—may cause your child to hold his hands over his ears and withdraw fearfully, especially if the sound is unexpected. This reaction is a remnant of a primitive reflex that has not been efficiently integrated into the child's nervous system yet—the Moro reflex, which is also known as the "startle response." (This reflex is typically seen during the first three to four months of life as an involuntary response to stimulation.)

On the other hand, this same child may not know his own voice, and may speak far too loudly or seek out noises that he *can* control. Too much visual stimulation may set him up to look away or avoid eye contact, yet he may also seek out the highly visual stimuli on smart phones, tablets, and computers. Obsessively watching ceiling fans, flicking lights on and off, and participating in other repetitive actions draw kids with sensory dysfunction into a visual world of their own. And self-stimulating behaviors, such as jumping in place, flapping his hands, and rocking are attempts to create some kind of inner organization and self-soothing.

Over- or under-reaction to any kind of sensory stimulation has the potential to set children up for misinterpreting the world around them and creating behaviors we don't like to see—including passivity or aggression, withdrawal from others, or temper tantrums. As adults, it's important to realize that those behaviors don't simply come out of nowhere. *Something* is almost always behind that behavior, setting the child up for a particular reaction.

Kids don't go out of their way to be bad or fail to understand what we want from them. Their behavior is shaped by their responses to the environment around them, both physical and emotional. When you're trying to understand that behavior—whether you are a parent, teacher, or physician—it's important to look backward to the events that led up to a particular moment and determine if there might have been a sensory issue that caused it. To assist you, let's take a closer look at each of our sensory systems, beginning with those with which you're most familiar.

The Visual System

The importance of the eyes in how they guide development cannot be underestimated. A newborn baby first discovers his outstretched hand through a primitive response known as the asymmetrical tonic neck reflex, ATNR, which helps connect her eyes with her hands. As neural development proceeds, the baby receives increasing information by watching the movement of her hand, prompting her to turn towards the visual stimulation she is receiving. This input into the eyes continues throughout life.

As children grow and develop, the eyes are a fundamental source of input into the cortex of the brain. If the developing child has a weakness in any of his other sensory systems, like the vestibular or proprioceptive systems, he can become over-reliant on visual input to tell him where he is in space. He might develop a very strong sense of visual dependence, over-relying on what he sees in an effort to draw additional information into his brain—a circumstance that can have both positive and negative results.

On the one hand, it's nice to have our eyes to guide us as we interact with and enjoy our visual world. But, on the other, this craving for visual stimulation can be waylaid by the visually distracting world we live in. What better source of visual distraction is there than a computer or television? And what happens if you are a young, developing child who requires sensory-rich physical input to create balanced neural pathways, but most of your time is spent looking at a two-dimensional iPad?

When a child overloads on visual stimulation without any physical connection to it, the experience is similar to the way in which drugs activate the brain—the visual stimulation becomes a stimulation on which she can become dependent. Ask anyone who has tried to wean a child off modern media devices without an accompanying emotional meltdown. Phones and tablets have become the modern "babysitter" for today's children, just as televisions were for previous generations. It's a common sight to see a two-year-old scrolling on his mother's phone for pictures or a game to play, yet this is *not* an excellent developmental tool, and does not add value to a child's developing motor skills, no matter how you look at it.

Remember: there is a very different experience between being licked by a puppy in your arms and looking at one on an iPad with the word "puppy" under it. A similar caution can be made about flashcards for young children. Reading, or more likely memorizing, a word at age one is not as important as snuggling up in a mother's lap and visually engaging in a game of peek-a-boo.

The visual system can also be easily over-stimulated in many children, and busy visual environments can greatly challenge kids. Bright lights, especially fluorescent lights, subtly flicker or pulse, and for kids who are hyper-sensitive to that repetitive visual stimulation, stress in the nervous system can be created. For some, this flickering of fluorescent lighting has even been shown to cause seizures.

Children who are under-responsive to visual stimulation can also behave in an atypical way. They may "disappear" inside themselves, seemingly tuning out everyone around them, choosing to self-soothe to find security in what they perceive as a chaotic environment. This is the kind of behavior you see in kids with autism—seen in the stereotypical socially withdrawn child who swings or rocks himself as he observes the environment around him out of the corner of his eye. It is as if the visual stimulation around him is too painful, or simply too much for him. Children with visual under-responsiveness may also be gravitationally insecure, possessing depth-perception issues that challenge them when they walk up or down stairs or lift their feet off the ground.

Children who avoid eye contact with others often do so because, for them, it's simply *too much visual input* to look someone else in the eye, a symptom of over-responsiveness. They observe the world via protective sidelong glances and may overly fixate on predictable static moving objects like wheels, flashing lights, or ceiling fans, all of which are activities that could set off developmental red flags to others. Some kids become obsessed with watching the movement of toys—the repetitive visual stimulation of watching a train go around and around a track can mesmerize them, taking them away from more interactive modes of learning and registering their environmental sensory input.

The Auditory System

The auditory system is a critically important system because it allows us to perceive language and communicate with others and is invaluable in interpreting the nuances or "meaning" of speech that are conveyed with pitch, frequency, and the intensity of sound. Without it, we must rely on other sensory systems in order to communicate, like vision or touch, but they are poor substitutes, especially when we get into school and must learn to negotiate through a new, more complex environment. Besides the obvious communication connection, the ability to hear helps protect us from potential dangers such as oncoming cars, or angry dogs.

If a child can't perceive sound accurately, it is obviously going to be a greater challenge for her to learn how to reproduce sounds and develop spoken language. Children who experience any degree of hearing loss, no matter how subtle, can have great challenges in communicating with others. Understanding the meaning of individual words and phrases, as well as linking thoughts and ideas to those phrases, contributes directly to the ability to hear and process information correctly.

Children who have hyper-acute hearing are often distracted by it, making it difficult to pay attention. They may also react very suddenly or fearfully to sounds the rest of us hardly notice, withdrawing from the sound as a means of self-protection. I have seen many children, for example, who have delayed potty training because of the associated fear they have of the sound of a flushing toilet. Some kids don't want to go to school because they fear that a fire alarm may suddenly go off, causing them to panic.

On the other side of the auditory spectrum are the children who are *hypo*sensitive to sound, in other words, kids who have a very hard time interpreting various sounds. For them, everything comes across as a kind of monotone jumble. Who wouldn't tune out that kind of input? They seem distractible simply because it's so hard to discern important auditory information from unimportant input. Paying attention in school settings is a huge challenge. After all, if the chatter of a classmate sitting next to you sounds no different from the words spoken by the teacher at the front of the class, how do you tune one out and tune the other in, and ultimately learn effectively in that environment? We perpetuate this kind of distraction with constant background noise from television, computers, music players, and conversations on mobile phones, and it's no wonder we see more of these kinds of issues in children today.

Language development can't help but suffer in kids with hearing issues, along with the development of their social skills. Children are frequently labeled as "difficult" because they fail to follow instructions—which they often simply cannot differentiate from the other conversations and noises going on around them.

A boy I recently observed in preschool had been born prematurely at twenty-six weeks (three and a half months early). Children born this early have critically underdeveloped nervous systems and require highly specialized neonatal intensive care in order to survive. This includes near-constant beeps and alarms made by various heart rate, breathing, and oxygen monitors. Every time they are touched, their oxygen saturation goes down, so even diaper changes or shifts in positioning can be too much for them, taxing their fragile systems. In many ways, the survival of the boy I was observing had depended on tuning out this sensory input, especially sound. Yet, when I was observing him, he was in a classroom with twelve other kids, trying to learn. His teacher expressed her frequent frustration over his lack of responsiveness to her directions and wanted to know how she could help him. I watched for an hour as she tried to get his attention, calling his name numerous times from across the room while he sat quietly on the floor and looked at a picture book.

All of the children in the room were making noise as they played, as preschoolers do. Loud music was playing in the background; kids were yelling on the playground just outside the window; and the door was open to the hallway where children from other classes were going to and from activities. There was no way this boy could hear the teacher calling his name, let alone learn optimally in that environment.

The cacophony of sound coming into his system was enough to fatigue even the most typical of children. He needed to be in a far less distracting environment, one that was truly quiet, to help focus his attention. His was a classic case of how easy it can be for a child's behavior to being misinterpreted, based on his reaction to his environment. It wasn't that he was purposefully failing to follow directions; he simply couldn't *hear* them.

The Tactile System

Our tactile system—the sense of touch—is our most-developed sensory system at birth, providing us with our first source of contact outside the womb. Our sense of touch literally allows us to grow comfortable in our skin. The largest organ in our body, our skin registers the distinctions between light and deep pressure, hot and cold, and sensations that are either pleasant and comforting or irritating and painful. Through the complex network of these tactile receptors, a baby is set up to bond with mothers, fathers, and caregivers as well as to connect with the physical world around him.

Kids who have a hypersensitivity to touch, in fact, have what we call "tactile defensiveness." They often have a hard time perceiving the nature, or intention, of touch by another person. By extension, if someone stands to close to them, or they are required to line up too closely to others in a line, they perceive that the person closest to them is intruding on their space, possibly even threatening harm. This is due to the close relationship between touch and the body's "fight or flight" response. Some kids who are hyper-sensitive to touch run from the perceived threat; others lash out with protective punches, and, unfortunately, kids with tactile defensiveness are often perceived as being combative, outcasts in the class, or bullies.

Tactile defensiveness can also be influenced by the misperception of touch received from the different textures that clothing provides. Think for a moment about the child who appears strangely sensitive to what he is wearing, or the one who gravitates to the same pair of pants every day. Clothing that seems utterly unremarkable to a hundred kids may drive another child wild with discomfort. Tags on the inside of shirt collars are notorious culprits, along with sock seams that ride up underneath their toenails. Some children attempt to cope with this challenge by insisting on wearing the same set of clothes day after day, while others can't wait to strip their clothes off as soon as they walk in the door at the end of the day. While treating this issue can take the skill of a therapist—and time—to resolve, quick fixes like cutting tags out of clothes and wearing socks inside out may help in the meantime.

Kids with hypersensitivity in their feet bounce along on their toes, especially when they are barefoot or on a potentially ticklish surface like grass or sand. Unfortunately, the more sensitive they are, the longer they might walk on their toes. While this may appear mildly cute when a child is little, prolonged toe walking can set a child up for trouble down the road. When this occurs over months or years, the tendons in the back of the legs (the "heel cords") can get overly tight, eventually requiring surgical correction. Anything you can do to avoid this pattern is going to be better for everyone involved. Even without reaching out for professional therapy, parents can help early on by encouraging their child to try activities like ice skating or roller skating to get their child's heels down to stretch and strengthen their Achilles' tendons. (If this doesn't work within six months time, working with a pediatric therapist to get to the root of the problem early on is highly recommended, before surgery becomes your only option.)

The child who presents himself as an extremely picky eater can be expressing another tactile defensive behavior. The mouth is filled with tactile receptors, which are highly sensitive to texture. There are many children who actually find the textures of various foods so disagreeable that they limit their diets to individual foods like macaroni and cheese or processed chicken nuggets or some other food their tactile systems can tolerate. When a disagreeable food or unwanted texture enters their mouths, it sets off "danger signals" that cause them to spit it back out. To avoid the discomfort they get from an "interior tickle" in their mouths, many kids suck on their shirts or other inedible objects. This seems to dampen the uncomfortable sensation they experienced from the food itself or can be used as a self-soothing mechanism. Sucking on a shirt, the corner of a blanket, or even a pacifier can be seen even in older children who have a hard time settling down or handling a busy environment.

It's important to remember to be careful about how you approach children with tactile defensiveness, whether they are showing signs of sensitivity in their mouths or the rest of their bodies. Something as simple as coming up behind a hypersensitive child and touching her lightly on the shoulder can cause a startle response or a full fight-or-flight reaction. Having their hair or face washed or nails clipped can be an equally prickly experience, and for some it's nothing short of excruciating.

As with the sense of hearing, we also see children with tactile hyposensitivity. These children *crave* touch because "normal" kinds of tactile experience simply aren't enough. Some children who are hyposensitive attempt to "feel" a world that's hard for them to connect to by touching everything—and everyone—they encounter. They may be insensitive to temperature, refusing to wear a jacket even when it's freezing outside, or they may fail to notice when they bruise or cut themselves. They may seek out the sensations that accompany falling down, rough-housing, pinching, and biting.

Hyposensitivity can manifest itself differently at different ages. As babies, some bang their heads on their cribs in an attempt to self-soothe, almost as if they are trying to release some unmet need inside. When they're a bit older, they may inflict unintentional pain on their parents, siblings, friends, or pets because they have such high pain thresholds themselves, and are unable to perceive touch adequately. Adolescents and adults may resort to some form of self-stimulation like masturbation or even overeating, in an attempt to fulfill some unmet sensation.

There are kids, too, who possess a *low* threshold to pain when their skin is touched, but at the same time experience a *high* tolerance to internal pain. These are the children who have a dampened response when they get physically hurt, yet dislike the feeling of being hugged. Over time this can contribute to cases of poor body image or an undeveloped sense of personal space.

No matter what the symptoms are of a disrupted tactile system, children who can't regulate this vital input suffer. Even without observing the extremes of tactile neglect that are so often present in orphanages around the world, we can see the impact on many kids' senses regarding their security and development. It is no surprise that children who are deprived of the comfort of being held at any age can view the world as a threatening or uncomfortable place.

The Gustatory and Olfactory Systems

It would be easy to assume that every child inherently loves to eat chocolate and ice cream, and that there really isn't much that can go awry with their gustatory system—their sense of taste. But the truth, as almost all parents discover, is that opinions of what tastes good vary widely in children (just as they do in adults), and that's one of the reasons parents encounter so many finicky eaters. But it's one thing for a girl to dislike broccoli, and another—with more severe sensory processing challenges—for a boy to refuse to eat anything other than French fries and chicken nuggets for years on end.

Some kids with food issues hate putting virtually anything in their mouths that is novel or untested; others seemingly need to taste and chew everything, whether it's candy, meat, shirt-tails, or even sofa cushions. These are the *hypo*tasters, kids whose brains don't successfully register taste sensations and who, in an effort to compensate, can become obsessive eaters or seekers of wanting input into the mouth (the kids who suck on their shirts or other inedible objects). As they get older, these kids become increasingly at risk for developing addictions to food, alcohol, cigarettes, or drugs, never fully satisfying their oral-motor taste buds.

Our olfactory sense—the sense of smell—is closely related to our sense of taste. As we all know, the aroma of a particular food or beverage can either attract or repel us. Anyone with an intact smelling system knows that the smell of a favorite food can prepare our digestive juices for a tasty meal ahead. And, although we seldom need to address specific olfactory problems in sensory integration therapy, a child's olfactory responses can color the way in which she integrates with the overall world around her.

Children who are picky eaters can often be encouraged to try a new food when they have had the opportunity to help out in the kitchen and to smell the food while it was cooking. This intermediate step of smelling goes directly into the brain via specific cranial nerves, helping her become more receptive to putting the unfamiliar food in her mouth. However, children with a tactile sensitivity towards food may also have a sensitivity to smell. This can contribute to well-developed defense mechanisms, which can quickly lead to the avoidance of eating. By engaging children in pleasant, cooking-related activities, making "food fun," this mechanism can often be bypassed, giving the child greater control and freedom to try something new. This will often lead to greater success in expanding the palate, rather than forcing him to try something new on his plate.

By encouraging a child to focus on how foods smell, you get one step closer toward the goal of her learning to tolerate lots of foods. At the same time, however, children who suffer *under*-stimulation of their olfactory systems often lack the discrimination to know when something should *not* go into their mouths—these are the kids who show little reaction to the smell of feces, rotten meat, or kitchen cleansers. Kids who are under-stimulated by aromas tend to try to smell or taste everything around them, whether dirt, modeling clay, or a messy diaper, because their brains don't receive the appropriate sensory cues they need to keep these things out of their mouths. For children without a sensitive olfactory system to protect them against ingesting items that can be poisonous or dangerous, their parents have to remain extra alert and cautious around the house.

The Vestibular System

The first system to be completely developed and operational in a young child is the vestibular system. No single sense is more important than the others, but the vestibular system plays a key role that affects them all, and is central to both learning and development. Our vestibular system allows us to deal with gravity; it affects balance as early as when a fetus begins to develop a sense of direction while floating in the womb. Once born, the real work begins when a boy moves his body for the first time, eventually gaining the strength to lift his head off a flat surface. The vestibular system is vital to learning and development— and it is also an area in which we focus sensory integration therapy.

The vestibular system controls our balance, our muscle tone, and our spatial orientation. Situated in the inner ear, the vestibular system consists of three fluid-filled canals that are set at right angles to each other. They respond to movement and changes in direction along with two fluid-filled vestibular sacs in the ear that additionally react to changes in head position and gravitational pull. Hair cells that line these structures are stimulated through motion and send nerve signals through the vestibular cochlear nerve in the ear directly to the cerebellum (the part of the brain that affects motor control and motor learning). The cerebellum receives this vital information from the vestibular system and then works to fine-tune it, allowing for coordinated movement and the development of motor skills. At the same time, auditory information goes from the ear to the language centers in the brain's cortex (where memory, attention, perceptions, and thoughts are also processed), while the cerebellum works to process information about where the body is in space. In addition, as this information enters the brain, whether through sound, movement, and/or vibration, it links up with the visual system. This further influences the development of visual motor skills, like handwriting and depth perception. Because of this complex inter-relationship, if any of these structures are out of alignment, then balance and coordination, speech and language, and reading and writing can all be affected.

Without a properly functioning vestibular system, every time we move our head we're at risk of losing our balance or losing our place on a page as we read. When a child can't move her eyes independently from her head (for instance, looking to the left while keeping the head facing straight ahead), the attempt to read can become very frustrating, and kids simply lose interest in trying to make sense of the words on a page. Without a properly developed vestibular system, it is also virtually impossible for a girl to visually track a ball that's thrown toward her and coordinate her body to catch it.

When sensory integration theory was developed by occupational therapist and educational psychologist Jean Ayers back in the 1960s, it was successfully argued that *many* children with learning disorders have symptoms of vestibular dysfunction, and in particular an absence of bilateral coordination, which is vital to the development and maintenance of muscle tone, body strength, and postural core stability. (Bilateral coordination is a function of the vestibular system that allows for both sides of the brain to talk to each other to produce coordinated movement.) In fact, vestibular input promoting adequate bilateral coordination is critically important for a variety of diverse skills, including being able to catch a ball, read a book, and even learn how to skip. Without appropriate vestibular functioning leading towards adequate bilateral coordination, children are inevitably delayed in developing movement skills that require using both sides of the body. They have difficulty in developing their postural control, as well as in developing the eye-hand coordination required for activities like playing ball and copying things off the board.

Bilateral synchronization also allows children to sit calmly in a chair, so they can focus on the task at hand, while crossing their midline with their eyes and hands, enabling them to develop strong motor skills with the smaller muscles in their hands. (Imagine an invisible line down the middle of the body. In order to read smoothly, your eyes have to be able to move from the left to the right. When there is a disturbance in crossing the body's midline, the entire head turns, contributing to a frequent loss in place when one attempts to read, leading to added frustration or inattention.) Without it, kids can't help but give in to gravity or get distracted—slouching over their desks, propping themselves up on their elbows, or wiggling around unconsciously. These children have little physical endurance, so they struggle when working on written tasks for long periods of time. When postural muscles are not working well together, it not only becomes significantly harder for the hands to manipulate small objects (like a pencil), but it also interferes with how the eyes are able to track visual input across the body's midline.

The vestibular system not only influences the motor control of the major muscle groups in the body, but it also affects how the throat, tongue, lips, and jaw work together in concert in order to produce intelligible speech. In addition to how one produces speech, this same system affects how the brain is able to process and organize speech. If there is trouble with the ears due to frequent ear infections or chronic fluid in them, this same system may have additional challenges identifying voices or discriminating between sounds. This, in itself, can be a huge source of distraction for anyone, so when the vestibular system is not working properly, requests may be easily misinterpreted, directions are misunderstood, and multiple instructions become next to impossible to follow in sequence.

Ultimately, kids with significant vestibular problems develop anxiety about the simplest elements of their daily lives—because *nothing* is simple, not even walking across a room. Depression can follow, because their bodies just don't feel good—*they* don't feel good in their bodies—so we focus intently on their vestibular systems as we treat sensory integration disorder, allowing them to have better integration within their bodies.

The Proprioceptive System

Our proprioceptive system is as little understood by ordinary people— and parents—as the vestibular system, yet its role in overall sensory integration is every bit as critical. The proprioceptive system is the neuromuscular system that allows us to know where our bodies are in space, as well as the system that allows us to understand where our arms and legs are in relation to each other and to our head. As an infant, we develop the motor patterns we need to keep our eyes level with the horizon through the workings of our primitive reflexes and—yes—our proprioceptive system. At the same time, we learn how to know where we are in relation to other people and how to unconsciously plan and execute movement.

As the proprioceptive system matures, we become able to make automatic movements and adjustments to our body position without conscious thought. We become fluid and lithe and are able to simply pick up a glass without having to think, "My hand is at my side and about three feet off the floor, so I'm going to open my palm, move my hand forward and up to the table, grasp the glass, and move it to my mouth." That astonishingly intricate series of events can unfold effortlessly thanks to our complex nervous system and our proprioceptive sense.

With this sense, growing children learn to perform thousands of everyday activities such as sitting in a chair, developing handwriting, becoming adept with a fork, and negotiating a crowded classroom without bumping into ten people or ten things. Our proprioceptive system helps us understand—automatically for most of us—how close to stand to someone in order to engage them without being so close that we're "in their face." Have you ever known someone who unremittingly stood way too close as she spoke with you? There is a very good chance that her proprioceptive system was at least a little bit out of balance.

Kids who lack a good sense of proprioception can appear to be rough. Lacking a sure sense of their body and its location in space, they gain information about where they are in space by throwing themselves onto other people or objects. They sometimes hurl balls far too hard or hurt people or pets without being aware of doing so, often covering their bodies with bruises that seem to appear out of nowhere. Children with poor proprioception tend to *over*-rely on their vision to compensate for this deficit—they have to compensate by using their eyes to show them where their bodies are, something that can consume lots of energy and cause them to fatigue easily.

These kids are easily distracted and struggle to negotiate their physical paths through life. They tend to trip over their own feet, quite literally bouncing off walls or crashing onto the floor or into their friends. It's not uncommon for a child with poor proprioception to fall out of a chair, land in a heap on the floor, and simply have no idea how the mishap occurred—and for her teacher or parents to assume she's acting out or simply not paying attention. These kids sometimes appear to be in constant motion as they attempt to orient themselves in space.

Others suffer "gravitational insecurity," exacerbated by underlying vestibular issues, and can become fearful when their feet are even just inches off the ground, not having the security of the physical input of the earth below them that their proprioceptive system interprets for them. Imagine how disconcerting that would be. When it comes time to sleep, they lie down in bed, but not only are their feet suddenly off the ground, next the lights go out, their vision is gone, and they feel like they're floating in space—and it *isn't* fun. This can lead to symptoms of anxiety (at best) or sleep disorders (at worst), and it's often the cause when a child stubbornly resists going to bed. If it is a serious case, toilets, chairs, and swings that lift children's feet off the ground can become similarly terrifying.

Poor motor planning, which facilitates the development of motor skills, can also occur as a result of proprioceptive dysfunction. Children can find it extremely difficult to "know" where their limbs and joints are in order to move them subtly and in concert, whether they are learning to ride a bike, catch a ball, write their name, or simply make their way across a classroom. These are the kids who get misinterpreted as troublemakers as they lumber down hallways with their heavy gaits, knock open doors, kick over chairs, plow into their friends, and seemingly break anything they touch—not because they're intentionally misbehaving or trying to get attention, but because they have a hard time controlling their bodies and using them sensitively and accurately.

When children develop normally, the vestibular and proprioceptive systems work in symbiotic combination with the other five senses to allow them to recognize and successfully use their bodies to accomplish a thousand things, both large and small. This allows them to grow confident and secure, and to engage themselves with the world around them. It's a process that begins in the first days following birth—as you will discover in the next chapter.

None of us ever reaches adulthood without encountering hurdles along the way. Some of us, as I've outlined here, face real challenges simply because we poorly process the sensory information that bombards us each and every day. But virtually all kids can ultimately fly—even those with sensory problems. And I'm eager to show you how.

CHAPTER 3

———•———

Understanding your child's developmental patterns . . .
Or, let's start at the very beginning

Like me, you probably remember the ecstasy—and the exhaustion—that accompanied your newborn's first days and weeks. When Alex was born, and when his brother, Max, followed four and a half years later, I was enthralled by what miracles those two tiny creatures so clearly were, overwhelmed with joy and love and the huge sense of responsibility that came with them. I'm sure that you, too, know those emotions, whether you've had one child or six.

You may have also noticed that changes begin to take place the moment your child is born, as he acclimates himself to the new environments around him. Your baby's brain is like a super-absorbent sponge, ready to make the most of every experience and sensation it can take in. Security, comfort, social, motor, and language experiences all play a part in this growth. Connections in the brain, known as "neural networks," allow babies to progress from the primitive reflex patterns they are born with to increasingly challenging and coordinated activities.

A baby's development during that first year of life occurs faster than at any other stage of development. During the first several months out of the womb, your newborn is rapidly adjusting to her new world, learning to regulate patterns of eating, sleeping, and breathing, cooing and crying to communicate, and becoming increasingly social and interactive through eye contact and visual tracking. By one month of age, a normally developing baby should clearly be able to hold your gaze for a couple of seconds. Within the first four to six weeks, most babies are starting to smile, at first reflexively, then intentionally.

Simply watching and interacting with your baby, capturing his gaze, and eliciting intermittent smiles is a vitally important way of developing a strong, bonded attachment. Babies love it when you talk and sing to them, as well as when you simply train your eyes on them and sigh in wonder while they snuggle in for a feeding. By three months of age, you will have heard your baby's first laugh, which will progress to a gleeful squeal by five or six months. At seven months, your baby will clearly know who you are, turning in response to your familiar voice. Remember, though, that not every child who develops learning challenges later on in childhood will demonstrate red flags as a baby. However, understanding normal development and knowing how to interact with your child early on can help pave the way for his optimal development.

As your child grows, eye contact continues to be critical not only in forming attachments, but also in driving sensory motor development. Encourage your child by looking for opportunities to capture his gaze, allowing him to imitate your expression or follow your face from side to side. When you hold your baby to feed him—whether from a breast or a bottle—he's at the perfect distance from your face to be able to engage it visually. Nothing's more stimulating to a newborn than your face, so forego all the toys intended to help capture your baby's attention—you've got the very best tool with you all the time.

Neurologically, children develop from their heads to their toes, then from their trunks to their fingertips. Notice how your baby must first lift her head off the mattress while on her tummy before she can isolate an arm to reach for a toy. Within her first six months, your baby progresses from a fully dependent being with little voluntary movement to an individual who can not only get her toes to her mouth but can also initiate her own movement. While on her tummy, she can lift her head up and turn it from side to side, while her feet kick up and down. By rolling, pulling her knees increasingly under her body and pushing off her knees, the beginning stages of crawling emerge. Soon she is pulling up onto her knees and then—far too quickly it may seem to some parents—she rises up to stand.

Head and Trunk Control

Whether born prematurely or at term, the American Academy of Pediatrics recommends that a newborn be placed on his back for sleeping to help prevent SIDS, Sudden Infant Death Syndrome. A guideline since 1992, it's been *very* effective in reducing the incidence of SIDS, but in turn we now see many more children than we once did who have misshapen heads, a condition called "plagiocephaly." In addition to plagiocephaly, developmental delays also seem to follow that are caused by the lack of experience in pushing up against gravity.

In other words, when an infant doesn't spend enough time on his tummy, he misses a critical opportunity in the development of bilateral coordination. This vital neurologic action is what integrates both sides of the body, paving the way for increasingly complex motor skills, as well as for reading and writing at school age. "Tummy time" is also what sets a developing baby up to crawl—an important milestone that we are seeing less and less of because parents are afraid to place infants on their tummies. In my experience, children need to crawl. In fact, I would much rather see a late walker than an early walker because that child almost certainly will have better bilateral coordination.

Tummy time is critical for a child to be able to strengthen the muscles of his neck, his shoulders, upper body, and trunk in order for him to crawl. By *one month of age*, your infant should be able to lift his head momentarily when he's lying prone; by *two months*, he should be able to lift and hold it at a forty-five degree angle; and a month later he should be able to hold it at ninety degrees. By changing the orientation of your baby's body—whether during feedings or diaper changes or in his bed—he will have the opportunity to turn his head evenly to both sides, decreasing the chance of developing torticollis—the shortening of muscles on one side of the neck.

One of the things that we see when babies don't spend enough time on their tummies is a tendency for them to resist that position as they grow. When they cry or fuss as they are placed on their stomachs, parents often think it's because their particular child simply "doesn't like it" and so they avoid it even more. Tummy time can be hard for some, yes, but it is an important developmental experience. In small children—as in some grown-ups—frustration is not a bad thing; it helps to drive development, and without it, we might not ever be inclined to move.

Please don't make the mistake of avoiding tummy time because your baby fusses in that position! Today, many babies spend far too much time in car seats or baby swings or some other kind of container that keeps them supported. For the same reason, you should not tightly swaddle a newborn for long periods. Though swaddling provides important warmth and security in a newborn's transition from the womb to the world, no child should be swaddled for the entire first five or six months of life. Instead, let your child move and experience life and discover on her own how to move her body and shift to new positions.

A typically developing child needs sensory input on both sides of his body—the front and the back. In order to develop a good foundation for bilateral coordination, tummy time is particularly important. By bearing weight on his hands, arms, and upper body, the small muscles in your baby's hands strengthen and allows for a greater variety of movements in the hands. This allows him to easily manipulate a small object—or a pencil in his hand—as he grows. Without this developmental step, writing suffers because the manual dexterity simply hasn't been developed.

As you may have guessed by now, I disagree with the current opinions of some in pediatric circles who say that crawling is not a necessary benchmark in development. While it's true that a baby does not *need* to crawl in order to walk, a child absolutely does need to develop the muscle strength and four-limb coordination that crawling so wonderfully provides in order to skillfully perform tasks requiring refined fine-motor skills later.

As a baby's head and neck strengthen at three or four months, neural pathways begin to develop away from his trunk and he increasingly begins to lift his head with arm support. He can now hold his head steady while he sits supported in your lap and turn his attention to events happening outside of your secure arms.

At three months, too, hands come together, an important milestone reflecting bilateral integration, setting the stage for appropriate neurologic development which will allow for advanced skills like reading and writing to emerge later in childhood. This same function of bringing the hands together allows a child to increasingly find his mouth and eventually hold his own bottle. By four months, this action becomes more intentional and functional, allowing him to reach out with each hand to either side of his body. A primitive reflex called the "palmar grasp" reflex allows him to grasp and shake a rattle and eventually bring it to his mouth. But don't be surprised if your young son doesn't release that rattle yet. It's not because he doesn't want you to have it, but because the primitive reflex that allows his to grasp it won't let him release it—yet.

Around four months is also the time when you don't ever want to leave a baby unattended on a changing table or even a king-sized bed, because although you may have never seen a hint of rolling activity till now, it's likely to begin when you least expect it. Most often, children flip from their tummy to their back first, rather than the other way around. If your child doesn't seem at all interested in rolling, try to encourage her by getting her to follow your gaze with her eyes onto her side. With practice and repetition, she'll be rolling from her back to her tummy by six or seven months.

A quick note: babies are also born with what's called the "stepping" reflex. As they are supported upright with their feet on the ground, they alternatively lift one foot and then the other and appear to "step" in place. Parents can be misled by this, thinking that their child is advanced in their development and sometimes try to encourage upright activities—but I strongly advise against this. Give your infants time, and don't overly encourage this upright maneuvering as preparation for walking.

By six months, as your baby's head, neck, and trunk strengthen, you should be able to pull her slowly from lying with her back on the floor to a sitting position without her head lagging behind. This will eventually lead to her being able to sit unsupported and transition on her own in and out of sitting. Protective reflexes will also emerge that will allow her to extend an arm rather than falling flat onto her side or back. Until you see this increased control, it is still important to protect her from an unwanted bump on the head by keeping close at hand or placing pillows around her for her to plop onto safely.

By about this same time, your baby's trunk control should have increased to the point where he can pivot his body in a circular motion, and even start to bring one or both knees forward under his body in preparation for crawling. Crawling backwards comes first, so don't be concerned—it happens because, frankly, it's easier. He'll be crawling forward within a month, an accomplishment you should be sure to savor because crawling is remarkably sophisticated, nurturing, and a vital neurological catalyst that supports the foundation of future development by stimulating millions of neurons to grow together into complex pathways. Because of this, children who skip the crawling stage may not have as solid of a sensory motor foundation that higher skills are dependent upon. This can set children up for "holes" in their development, making more advanced actions like reading and writing more of a challenge later on, so—long story short—don't be in a hurry for your child to walk.

A parent once came to our clinic because her five-month-old daughter had terrible torticollis and reflux (a condition marked by frequent spit up). The tightness in her neck had begun to appear at about six weeks of age, and the reflux followed soon afterwards. When I asked how she spent her time, I found out that she spent most of her time in a car seat, baby carrier, or baby swing, almost always facing in the same direction. When her mother held her, she kept her swaddled tightly, mistaking her daughter's crying for just being tired or having an upset stomach. The mother was afraid to put her daughter on her tummy due to the vociferous crying protest that ensued. I explained to her that developmental specialists have created the term "container babies" to describe children who have limited movement experiences early on. Many of these kids encounter developmental challenges from their lack of movement, and—without question—are set up for a multitude of problems later on as a result.

The mother had heard from a friend about how CranioSacral Therapy can help with reflux and head shape, which certainly sounded like a better option for her daughter than being forced to wear a cranial helmet to correct the increasing flattening in the side of her head (plagiocephaly). Yet, what this little girl was experiencing might have been completely avoided if only her parents had understood the importance of allowing her to spend time outside of being contained or swaddled, while incorporating tummy time with good positioning early on. Fortunately, we were able to begin working with her daughter and, before long, with the help of some physical therapy, better positioning, and CranioSacral Therapy, her reflux went away. Soon she was tolerating tummy time without a glitch and her head shape eventually became normal.

The Swirl of Technology

One of the most important aspects of early childhood development is an infant's visual discovery of the variety and complexity of the world around him. If a baby seldom gets to move, and is always positioned on his back, then he doesn't get to take big looks at everything surrounding him. If he isn't allowed to engage visually and have a variety of visual experiences, it's very difficult for him to develop eye-hand connections and an ability to attach with others. Yet, if he gets *too much* visual stimulation without the ability to move in response to it, this can be equally—if not even more—damaging to his overall nervous system.

I can't help but observe a correlation between rising rates of ADHD and autism and young children's increasing use of tablets and smart phones. It is shocking how very young children today—even babies—are passively receiving major doses of visual stimulation in two-dimensions, instead of three. I encounter far too many youngsters who prefer to interact with a television, tablet, or computer screen instead of with their parents, siblings, or peers. Computer games and videos designed for infants and very young children easily overstimulate visual pathways in developing nervous systems. While this may seem like a good idea to keep them quiet or passively entertained for a time, it also keeps them from absorbing critical information from their environment and interacting with others.

I believe there is a direct correlation between this type of sensory input and kids who don't pay attention to others and, as a result, develop poor social skills. The over-stimulating visual input acts like a drug on their young nervous systems, and this excitation of their brains occurs without the critically important *physical* connection to their bodies that good development demands. This stimulation—disembodied in a very unnatural way—is a potent drug, and we are only just beginning to see the developmental ramifications it's causing.

I recently saw an advertisement for a potty-training seat that actually had an electronic tablet mounted on it. It was being marketed to busy parents who liked the idea of turning potty training over to a computer software application that purportedly would both instruct and entertain their child—a scary concept, if you think about having an electronic device in lieu of a parent teaching their child. There is *nothing* better for a young child than direct interaction with a parent or another person, whether it is at the dinner table or over a potty chair. Person-to-person connections are critically important in every child's development. I don't believe that it is a coincidence that disorders in which children are fixated visually with limited interpersonal connections are increasing so rapidly in a world enthralled with technology. Many suffer unintentionally from their parents' misguided idea that a computer game can make a child "smarter" in some way. Movement and physical connections are absolutely vital in early life, especially for learning. Without active participation in the world around the developing child, the greatest opportunities for typical growth and development can be easily missed.

While technology is a great advantage to most of us, I strongly suspect that we are creating a *dumber* population as a result of it. Life is becoming too depersonalized. People text each other now instead of picking up the phone to call, and every day I see dozens of parents and babysitters pushing babies in strollers while talking on their phones as they make their way down the street. And you know yourself how many kids in restaurants are commonly handed their parents' phones or tablets to keep them quiet at the table.

I know I'm a bit of a crusader regarding toning down our reliance on technology, but it's because I know from lots of professional experience how much good early development—or its absence—can affect children throughout their school years, and even for the rest of their lives. Forget baby videos and their ilk. Entertain your child with peek-a-boo and patty-cake instead of lights and sounds on a bright screen. Make funny faces with your infant child; play airplane games with him. Moving, playing, and discovering are essential elements of a child's journey.

Day Care . . . Dealing with Reality

Because in so many young families these days both parents need to work at jobs outside their homes, spending quality developmental and bonding time with their infants is all the more important. Many moms have to return to work just six or eight weeks after their baby is born. Newborns often have to be shuttled off to day care, where they are likely to spend excessive time in car seats (dubbed "containers" by developmental experts) even when awake—to allow their caretakers to look after the needs of a number of other children at the same time.

If you are considering day care for your child, make sure to visit the facility first and pay attention to your intuition as you observe. How much human interaction will your baby be receiving if she spends many hours a day there? How much movement will she have the opportunity to experience? Day care is a situation that's far from ideal, yet it's very common. A recent Harvard study demonstrated that the neglect of an infant—even unintentional neglect—can actually be more harmful than overt physical abuse. The bottom line is that no matter what the demands are on your time, it is important for you—as well as for others who care for your baby—to find a way to spend as many precious moments as you can with your baby. Watching TV and having passive interactions are poor substitutes if you are trying to develop a safe, enriching, interactive world for your child in which to grow.

Becoming Social

Our children are born into a naturally social world. During the first couple months of life, infants spend most of their time sleeping, getting used to life outside the womb. Even in utero, there is evidence that suggests that our babies are reacting to input going on around them. I recommend that you engage in every opportunity you can to build a bond with your child and communicate, both verbally and nonverbally, even from the very beginning in order to foster the beginning of that social development. When you're feeding your baby, talk to him, look him in the eye, smile at him, and tell him he's wonderful. Sing to him, coo with him, marvel at the moment and the singular blessing of those interactions.

Very young babies typically do not engage in interactive play with other infants. Developmentally, they are simply not neurologically programmed for that kind of social interaction. Until children reach two, three, or even four, they normally engage in what's called "parallel" play—exploring the world by themselves, often in a room filled with others their age who are exploring on their own, as well.

Yet, somewhat paradoxically, those first couple of years are also vitally important for developing strong emotional attachments—for learning how to connect and how to love. The paradox is one you can easily observe in a pasture that is filled with horses, yet in which a newborn foal stays as close as it possibly can to its mother. Infant humans, too, need an anchor—one person (or two people) who stay very close at hand to help them feel secure in their environment so that they can explore it freely. It's only when they understand that their anchors are rock solid and always dependable that babies (whether human or equine) become secure enough to begin freely exploring and interacting with others—which is a major developmental step that cannot occur until that anchoring is a given in their lives.

It's important to observe how your child interacts with other babies, other toddlers, and other children no matter what his age. This can give you critical cues into how your child is beginning to view the world and get along with others. Does he prefer to be with adults—who are more "predictable," let's say, than most kids are? Because adults seem so steady by comparison, children who have underlying anxieties or fears, or who simply find it difficult to interact with their environment, often gravitate toward familiar and comfortable adults from whom they receive comfort and support—normally a mom or a stay-at-home dad, or whomever they view as their chief "protector."

By the time a child reaches two, he should be recognizing other kids around him, learning what's "mine," and how to say "no!"—in essence establishing his territory, creating boundaries, and setting limits. It's at this point that parenting begins to be as much about shaping your child's socialization as maintaining his physical health and development. Teaching your child how to share, how to refrain from hitting or biting when she seeks something she wants, and how to be cooperative instead of selfish are tasks that require gentle reinforcement and constant modeling to create behavioral patterns that can endure.

Seeking Assistance

Let me offer you some very straightforward advice: If you have a nagging doubt about your child's development—either now or in the future—seek help. Parents who have children with emerging sensory processing issues often face particular challenges in socializing their kids. Listen to your "gut." Ask yourself, is this behavior "typical" compared to other children his age?

As your youngster's foremost advocate, it's vital for you to be a realist about the situation you and your child face—being in denial about what's going on is *never* helpful. If you think something might be wrong, start by talking to your child's pediatrician, teachers, babysitters, and other caregivers about how they think your child is doing compared to other kids they observe.

I'm not suggesting that you go looking for trouble, but do seek input from others who perhaps can observe things that you find hard to see. Most often, parents will be the first to wonder if something is "not quite right." Listen to your internal questioning and seek some answers. It's always invaluable to learn how your child relates to others in environments where he's away from you. Kids behave differently when their parents aren't with them—it's a fact that every pediatric therapist is very attuned to—and the more information you have about the range of your child's behaviors in novel environments, the better.

Normally, the logical first step in looking for assistance is to raise an issue with your child's pediatrician. If you have a pediatrician who is attuned to child development issues and the benefits of therapy, she can help you sort out whether your child can be helped with early intervention. Yet, remember that many pediatricians have no background or experience with the specifics of modalities used in physical and occupational therapy practices, like sensory integration or CranioSacral Therapy; they simply may not be aware that there are lots of physical and occupational therapists who can offer your child remarkable kinds of help. I also advise that, if your child's doctor suggests that you simply wait six months to see if an issue resolves itself, you should do a little research on your own.

The danger of waiting is that it just puts you six months, or more, behind the time when your child can benefit most. Remember how quickly a child develops early on; it is best to jump on that developmental train and get things moving in the right direction before bigger problems occur. As I've said, listen to your gut. You already think the potential for a problem is significant enough that you've thought about raising your concerns with your pediatrician, after all. And six months is a long time. One of the true constants in my thirty-five years as a therapist is the reality that the earlier kids get help, the faster they are able to get on the right track and avoid rough patches down the road.

By the time a child is *four, five, or six years of age*, she should be learning quite well how to get along with other kids. She should be excited to have other children be part of her environment, learning how to give and take, and developing friendships and a real desire to spend time interacting with her peers.

As I described in the last chapter, some children who walk into or push others over aren't being "mean," they're trying to receive sensory stimulation that they otherwise lack. These children don't perceive touch in the way their peers do, and for many of them it's hard to understand that biting or kicking hurts, because to them it doesn't. I'll never forget a little boy who was almost four who was on the verge of being kicked out of preschool. The first thing he would do when he came into school in the morning was to give his teacher a big hug. This initial deep pressure allowed him to feel secure enough to not be bothered by others for the first twenty minutes of class, but as soon as the pace picked up, he started hitting his friends. Adding some intermittent "pressure breaks" with a mini trampoline in the class solved the problem in class, while he could work on developing more appropriate neural pathways in his therapy.

If early behavioral issues that are clearly sensory related don't get addressed appropriately, they will almost inevitably lead to significantly bigger problems down the line. Fortunately, for this little boy they did not. But what should you do if things don't appear to be progressing as they should for your child?

Inevitably, a parent's relationship with her child is different from that of a teacher, therapist, or even friend, and sometimes the more distanced perspective of a trusted friend or adviser can be very helpful. For the same reasons, in therapy, a child needs someone outside of the family circle who will push him beyond what he would necessarily undertake on his own and help him build on his every success. When I finally acknowledged that my son, Alex, needed therapy as a young boy, I knew I couldn't be both his mom *and* his therapist.

We parents tend to be overly protective of our kids, even when we know better, because we are our children's champions—it's part of our nature and would be a fundamental part of our job description if we had one. We want to make the world a safe place for our kids, and we try to be the best parents we possibly can be. Having someone else take a fresh look at your child and support and encourage her—allowing her to start really believing in herself and her capabilities—can make a huge difference in her life.

In the same way, checking in with other people about how your child is progressing can give you some excellent insight—particularly if you can avoid becoming upset if they tell you something you don't like. Some will insist that the sky is falling all around your child and that you're blind to the crisis, but you don't have to *believe* what others say; simply register the input and look for patterns that may begin to emerge when you hear comments from a number of people. Be aware, too, that lots of folks will try to calm your fears by brushing off your concerns. Again, add this opinion to your list, but don't carve it in stone.

An overly-involved grandparent who insists that she has all the answers and that you're parenting "all wrong" is just as obstructive as the other grandparent who always reminds you, "Oh, Johnny was just like that when he was Jason's age. It's nothing to worry about. Trust me, I know. The boy will be fine."

Your best friend may make light of a situation and try to brush off your concerns, often because she wants *you* to feel good (and, perhaps, because *her* child is showing similar patterns). Remember: nobody *wants* to tell a friend that they think something is wrong with their child. Most people's natural tendency is to protect and attempt to make everything okay by not bringing problems to another person's attention. It's far easier for me, a trained therapist, to say, "Your child has a problem," than it is for a friend or relative. Therapists are valuable precisely because they are *not* friends or family—as well as because of their extensive training and professional expertise.

Early intervention does not mean that your child will never have future problems, however. We *all* have issues that come and go in our lives. Although they can be hard to sort out at times, by being proactive and addressing red flags early, you have the potential to save yourself—and especially your child—a lot of anguish and therapy time in the long run.

The Next Steps

There are lots of different options out there for how and where to seek help for your child if you are concerned about his development or learning. If you don't feel your pediatrician is attuned enough to your child's issues—or experienced enough with therapies designed to help overcome them—one option is to ask for a referral to a specialist.

Developmental pediatricians and pediatric neurologists are both doctors who are well versed in the variety of developmental and neurological issues that children can be faced with. However, keep in mind that many traditional physicians who diagnose developmental disorders are trained to focus on medication as a means of alleviating them.

If you visit a pediatric physical therapist or occupational therapist who is specifically trained in sensory integration theory and treatment, on the other hand, she will evaluate your child and offer you a physical treatment plan. Because of this difference in treatment planning, this is often the most holistic place to begin treatment, and a physical or occupational therapist can provide your physician with invaluable information about your child's developmental patterns.

One of the goals of a complete developmental evaluation is to establish what those developmental patterns are and suggest what's likely getting in your child's way, as well as to provide some options for the best way to help set things straight. On the other hand, if you repeatedly postpone or avoid seeking out an evaluation, you might not recognize that you have a fixable problem in front of you until it becomes a big one.

A good evaluation includes a checklist or overview of your child's developmental pattern to date. Even if you have a hard time remembering when your child crawled or stood up for the first time, the more information you can provide, the better. Every detail provides insights into your child's individual pattern. A sensory profile that you can complete provides invaluable information on how your child perceives and reacts to the world around him. Patterns of strengths and weaknesses can be gleaned from this profile as well, further alerting therapists to the systems that appear to be the most involved.

Specific sensory integration-based developmental testing should only be performed by pediatric physical and occupational therapists trained specifically in sensory integration theory and practice. The tests that are used will depend on your child's age and the challenges he is exhibiting. There are a variety of assessment tools available to therapists, and every therapist has favorites. Ideally, therapists will want to see how each child does on a standardized test, looking at very specific criteria that tell us where the child falls in his motor development, compared to other children his age.

In these standardized tests, specific directions are given to the child to see if she can follow through with a particular action. Some examples are: Can your daughter stand on one foot with her hands on her waist for five seconds without bending more than twenty degrees? Can your son hit a specific target by moving his arm up and over his shoulder to accurately throw a ball from seven feet away? How fast can your child run fifty feet, then pick up an object and run back? These kinds of tests examine your child in a very standardized fashion—that's why they are so valuable.

When a parent simply tell us, for example, that her daughter can balance on one foot, it might actually mean that she can balance on one foot, but only with assistance or in a "non-standardized" fashion. There are actually a number of different ways to balance on one foot, in fact (extending your arms out to the side, bending at the waist, or even sticking one foot out in a quick and cockeyed motion for a couple of seconds). These are all very different and require less postural control than standing upright with your hands on your waist, lifting a knee up, and holding it in balance for six seconds, which is the style that would be required with standardized testing.

As a parent, you're not likely to pay much attention to those distinctions—but an evaluator certainly will. It is, literally, the evaluator's job to observe your child's developmental abilities and milestones in the most objective light possible. This objectivity provides professionals with a vital starting point from which to measure your child's progress. By measuring it against the normative actions and behaviors of thousands of other children, we collectively come to understand your child in ways you alone can't otherwise know her. Armed with the results of a thorough and careful evaluation, you and the professionals assisting you can then jointly decide the very best subsequent steps.

Keep in mind that not every child who is evaluated requires therapy. The therapist may well recommend other activities to try first. On the other hand, if you and the team of professionals advising you collectively decide that your daughter *could* benefit from therapy, the very good news is that the therapy will likely be of great benefit to her. In either case, you'll have the benefit of guidance from a developmental specialist about what course of action might be of the greatest immediate benefit to your child—whether that "treatment" includes home exercises, a sports program, or a regimen of therapy that will really help your young child fly!

CHAPTER 4

---·---

How to be your child's advocate . . .
What to do to get the help you need

Jeffrey was two and a half when I met him, the adopted son of a prominent attorney and his wife. When his parents first took custody of him as an infant, they accepted him as perfect, just as we all do after counting our newborns' fingers and toes. However, as Jeffrey grew, he became increasingly fixated on fans and toy trains rather than on his parents' faces, and they began to suspect that something was not quite right. By two years of age, it was obvious that Jeffrey was perceiving the world differently than their friends' children were.

Jeffrey's parents took him to a pediatric neurologist who confirmed their fear that he had autism. She advised them to start therapy immediately, and before they had even left her office they had called to arrange for an appointment. Like many parents in similar situations, the realization that their fears were valid left them in a panic.

When they first brought him in to see me, I remember being struck by what a beautiful child Jeffrey was. He had big brown eyes, rosy cheeks, and a head full of curls. He appeared to be a thick, sturdy child, but when I lifted him onto a swing his body melted into mine, feeling more like a marshmallow than a rambunctious two-year-old. He was floppy, like a rag doll, with very low muscle tone, and he had essentially no language. His anxiety level was initially off the charts, with eyes as wide as saucers as he observed the world passively around him. Virtually everything he encountered for the first time worried or frightened him, and he would freeze in a kind of "non-response."

Later, as he learned to talk, his anxiety manifested itself into dozens of repetitive questions, as if he were trying his hardest to convince himself that the new object in front of him was safe.

Children who are born with recognized disabilities generally begin to receive help from pediatric specialists almost immediately. The Individuals with Disabilities Education Act (IDEA) ensures that they can receive services throughout the nation, and governs how states and public agencies can provide early intervention, special education, and related services to more than 6.5 million eligible infants, toddlers, and children who have disabilities—regardless of whether their parents have the means to pay for services.

It's often a different story for kids like Jeffrey who appear perfectly normal at birth, yet whose developmental issues have the potential to cause trouble in the months or years ahead. Too many of these children only receive attention from their parents and teachers once it's clear that something isn't quite right—if they get the care they need at all. Many other children, whose difficulties are not acknowledged, proceed through school being called "lazy" or "unmotivated" as their self-esteem plummets. Bright children stop trying because they know they should be able to do better but they just can't seem to get it together.

Issues that arise when a child is in first or second grade—such as pronounced difficulty with handwriting—can be linked back to the likelihood that they walked too early or that they never crawled. I recently spoke with a gentleman in his seventies who told me how he had never crawled and had only recently realized what a problem this had been for him. He had been an avid golfer throughout his life, and had successfully developed his own style to compensate for the challenges that skipping the developmental stage of crawling had created for him. Not long before we spoke, he had begun a program that addressed many of the same issues we take on with the children we see. Even as an adult, later in life, he was delighted with the changes he was observing in his memory, attention, and focus.

Being aware of developmental challenges—and knowing how best to support your child through them—can make a huge difference in her ultimate success and how she feels about herself. Educating yourself to know whether your child is demonstrating a characteristic that's simply unique to her, or whether she is facing a true developmental challenge and needs help is vital. If you have a nagging doubt about how she is doing—let's say you're seeing a bit too much anxiety or a little too much frustration, or she's avoiding activities that her friends seem to love—take a long, objective, and unworried look at her. Investigate. Do not run away from the issue or assume that it is "nothing." Many times, it is something that is very easy to fix—when it's addressed early. Our children don't come with an instruction manual, and the best way to ensure that they develop as fully and joyfully as possible is by becoming their strong and steadfast developmental advocate.

Important Questions

When you think your child is displaying troubling signs, the first thing you should do is ask yourself several important questions.

First of all, what are the patterns you are seeing? Does your son seem to have a "pattern" of sensitivities, like being a picky eater, or cringing in response to loud sounds, or can he only sleep with a sound machine or a light on? Carefully examine the patterns of those sensitivities. Read books. Investigate on the Internet. Talk to your friends. Develop a sense of whether those differences are extreme or relatively minor. As you might guess, in many instances, this becomes easier to discern once your child enters school, because there are many other kids with which to compare him, and teachers are often the first ones to point out important concerns. It can be hard when you're a parent at home and only have your own experiences to rely on, but it is important to not wait too long if you have a concern. Every child is different, so be realistic about how your child appears to be learning and how he handles challenging situations or transitions. For example, very bright children are great at masking their reactions to difficulties, and can often appear emotional, demanding, manipulative, or strong willed when the source of their problems is actually a kind of traffic jam piled up in their brains.

These behavior patterns often start subtly and are unintentionally reinforced when a parent feeds into the behavior by giving it attention. Remember that all attention is equal in the mind of a child—negative as well as positive. Children learn very quickly where and how they get the most attention and will repeat the patterns that bring that attention to them most consistently. Nature very wisely programs us into thinking our children are perfect—because they *are*; they are absolutely perfect at being who they are. But, when they begin to develop in ways that interfere with how they learn, you can get the help they need and set them up for greater success as they continue to grow, develop, and learn.

Is your child sleeping well? Does he wake often during the night? He may have poor sensory regulation. Does he snore? He may have enlarged adenoids. Does he worry about everything? He may have severe anxiety. Poor sleep can be a huge factor in a child's behavior, and his ability to learn and develop complex physical and mental skills. How about eating? Does she only eat macaroni and cheese or pizza? A varied diet rich in vitamins, nutrients, and omega acids is essential for a developing brain. Food allergies can cause stress and anxiety, as well. All these factors can additionally influence a child's behavior and ability to learn. Interestingly, individuals with food sensitivities often seek out those same foods, causing an irritation or allergy. Current research is examining what comes first—whether an allergy is always present, or whether the ingestion of too much of one food can cause children to actually develop an intolerance for that food. (Nutrition is a complex science, and its importance cannot be discounted. We all know that "we are what we eat," and there is no question that good nutrition is vital for the developing brain and body of the child.)

Only a decade or so ago, many pediatricians claimed that calorie intake was the sole nutritional issue meriting much attention. As long as a child was gaining weight, her diet was fine, they presumed. But we know now that how and what a child eats absolutely does affect her ability to process information, think, and fully develop her brain. Consulting with a well-trained, licensed nutritionist who specializes in children is a good place to start if you are worried about your child's eating habits. Or, if your child is a picky eater, consulting with an occupational or speech therapist who understands sensory sensitivities and is experienced with feeding issues can help.

How is your child doing in comparison to accepted standards? Pay close attention to the developmental milestones and benchmarks which are available to you. They are important guides in helping you accurately determine your child's progress. Everyone develops a bit differently—which can be a challenge to measure at times—but watch how your child does things. Is she crawling primarily using one side, or is she not crawling at all? Is she delayed? Does her movement look funny? If you are worried, have a developmental specialist check her out.

As we've discussed, kids who don't spend any time on their stomachs can often encounter problems. This position is critical to a baby's development. It provides sensory input into the baby's front side and allows him to develop his head, neck, and postural muscles. Without tummy time, learning to roll and cross over the middle of the body can become a significant obstacle. Babies who have little tummy time sometimes develop so much tightness in their back muscles that they go directly to standing and walking, and in doing so they forego the important development of their eyes and hands and the bilateral coordination that is important for many activities, including reading and writing.

When a child misses the important input that comes from crawling, problems tend to emerge, affecting his ability to sit still in a chair, write legibly, or play sports with ease. That isn't to say that the problems will necessarily become serious, but they can present themselves in ways that certainly make things much harder for children later. Paying attention to developmental milestones and ensuring that your child doesn't "skip" them is a fundamental part of acting as an advocate for your quickly growing child.

Your Social Child

Your child's emotional development is as important as her physical development. How does your son feel about himself? Does he smile easily? Is your daughter a very serious girl? Does she communicate easily? Does your son appear uncomfortable with other children his age? Is he drawn to the heavy visual stimulation offered by a tablet computer rather than interaction with other kids or adults?

Each of us is born with a unique temperament. We're all different in that regard, and that fact is much of what makes interacting with others throughout our lives such a wondrous experience. You don't want to try to "change" a child with an inherently serious temperament, yet it is critically important for your child to be comfortable in her skin, to be able to interact with other people, and to develop cooperative skills and empathy. If your child is something of a "loner," be particularly careful in regulating her exposure to media and technology, and foster positive face-to-face interactions with others in every way you can. Bullying and social isolation can be extremely damaging to a child, especially when those issues are not addressed, early on.

A key aspect of advocacy is to be sure that *you* are as present as possible for your child. Are you constantly texting, working or browsing at your computer, talking on the phone, or watching television? We live in a high-tech and readily distracting world that can easily take us out of the moment that is before us. It is worth examining our own habits and how they might affect others, most particularly our own children. It is almost impossible to be present if you are busy sending a text message or checking your email. Your child *needs* you—not just to dress and feed him and make sure he gets enough sleep. You are your child's role model, whether you realize it or not. Starting with the very first eye contact the two of you make, your child pays enormous attention to what you do and how you do it, patterning his behavior after yours.

It is not unusual to see very young children holding a phone to their ear or pushing buttons on the television remote, as you know. Learning to entertain himself with a hand-held phone becomes a game of instant gratification as changing shapes, colors, or cartoon characters dance across the screen with a push of a button. I have seen parents beam as their two-year-old swipes the screen to see pictures float by. At first glance, this may seem like the perfect pacifier to entertain a child while a parent focuses his attention elsewhere—after all, the child is quiet and entertained while the parent accomplishes an important task. But something else is also going on. When you look closer, you see a child being subtly encouraged—and even trained—to withdraw into himself and not connect with others. A two-dimensional screen becomes more important than you are in that moment.

As I have already suggested, you should not confuse focus on a two-dimensional screen as a substitute for quality personal interactions with others. This kind of visual stimulation is as potent as a drug, stimulating visual pathways with no sensory motor connections to anchor them. It's a very different experience to look at a picture of a pinecone on an iPad, compared to holding one in your hands. To feel its prickliness, its weight, its stickiness, and to smell it, rather than just connecting it to a label "pinecone" under it. Connections between people are critical for a child's development and it's up to you to make those opportunities available to your child.

Off to School

Virtually all of us live very fast-paced lives these days, and it's easy to get caught up in the vortex of everything moving *quickly*. As part of that acceleration, children go off to school far sooner than they once did. Because I was a working mother, my children attended day care and "mother's day out" programs from the very beginning. My second child was in school by the time he was sixteen months old—although starting school so early had been unheard of when I was a girl. While there are certainly advantages to early socialization and being exposed to a variety of experiences outside the home, there are disadvantages as well. Parents and children are all affected by this early schooling trend. As young children integrate into school and turn their focus away from home for the first time, parents take the opportunity to turn to their careers and other interests, which might have been ignored for a stretch of time. This sets up the tendency to over-indulge the children, or to set loose limits for them, when they finally do spend time together. Unfortunately, this well-intentioned action can lead to anxious and demanding children.

Although it's impossible to reshape the whole society in which we live, we can find ways in our own lives to slow the pace and ensure that there is plenty of down time. We all know parents who follow their children's full day of school with piano, karate, swimming, team sports, then tutoring—afraid that if they don't schedule these extra activities, their kids won't be able to attend the best school. Teachers and after-hours school programs send even very young children home with hours of homework, yet there is no evidence that hours of homework by itself makes kids smarter or gets them into the college of their parents' dreams. And what improper amounts of homework can do is set up a pattern of frustration and aversion to what you want most for them: learning, experiencing, loving life, and interacting appropriately with others. It's vital for kids of every age to have unstructured time in which *nothing* is expected or has to happen, but in which something inevitably does, whether it's a board game, a walk in the park or on the beach, staging a backyard play, or simply being silly. These activities are very different from doing endless work sheets, or sitting mindlessly in front of the television or latest computer game.

To be the best advocate for your child, be aware of what is going on in school. Talk to the teachers, hear what they have to say about your child, and always keep in mind your child's total developmental picture. With school starting at such an early age today, fine-motor activities are often pushed on children before they are developmentally ready for them. We see this with handwriting, when kids as young as three are introduced to writing their letters. Children at this age are still developing their core musculature, their attention centers, and their abilities to use their eyes and hands in concert. When teachers put pencils in their hands and expect them to carefully shape letters and words, inefficient patterns tend to emerge and get in the way of how the child is actually able to write. It's no wonder their hand fatigues quickly and resistance to writing sets in.

When children are pushed too fast, too early—before their bodies have sufficiently developed to allow them to accomplish what we want them to do—we set them up to believe that learning is a struggle and that school is *hard*. As adults, we have learned that much of life *is* a struggle; frustration drives development to a certain degree, and scientists agree that a bit of stress is a good thing. Yet stress at a very young age primarily creates anxiety. Putting a child under chronic stress is a recipe for disaster, both developmentally and when trying to nurture self-esteem. As your child's advocate, you need to just say "no" to grandparents, friends, and schools that insist that your five year old needs the same kinds of pressure to perform and achieve as a college student.

Brothers and Sisters

If there are siblings in the family, a whole new set of challenges can emerge. Older children often feel abandoned when a newborn needs their parents' attention. The youngest members of the family suffer as well, often stuck in car seats while Mom is shuttling an older brother or sister from one activity to the next.

Have you ever heard a mother say that her second son is "like her first son in every way"? Of course you haven't. Nature dictates, in fact, that each child in a family appears unique from the outset. Just when you think you finally have parenting figured out with your first child, along comes a second and with her comes an entirely new set of issues, concerns, and problems. The only solution is to treat each child as the individual she truly is. The school that is perfect for your eldest may be entirely wrong for your second child. And if your oldest daughter is crazy for sports, you might as well prepare for the possibility that her younger brother will find nothing in life so interesting as books. Let your children show you who they are, and pay close attention. Support their unique interests, skills, and challenges. Say yes to what intrigues and delights them, and watch their self-esteem grow. If you have a child who appears fearful and limited in his interests, gently present new opportunities and be careful to set him up for success by not pushing too hard—or giving up too easily. Do so not only because you love him, but because you're his advocate in his early life and he needs your help in every way.

Early Intervention

It's important to know that if you suspect that something is not quite right with your child, especially during your child's first decade of life— if she is exhibiting any kind of developmental or motor delay—there are programs available to help. Every state offers a federally funded Early Childhood Intervention Program (ECI) than can help to sort out significant developmental disabilities well before you child's school years commence. The 1990 Individuals with Disabilities Education Act (IDEA) gives each state the authority to create its own program, while complying with federal IDEA requirements.

A program called Child Find is available to families with a child under three years of age who may have developmental issues. Your city's public school system should be able to connect you to Child Find, which, in turn, will link you to assistance from ECI, or your own state's equivalent program. If your child is *older* than three, he may be eligible for the Preschool Program for Children with Disabilities, PPCD. Be aware that many of these programs require that your child has a developmental diagnosis placing him below the twenty-fifth percentile in physical performance or behavior compared to his peers in order to qualify for services.

There are *many* developmental diagnoses in which kids don't fall that far behind but, nonetheless, they can certainly benefit from therapeutic services, so some referral systems do have drawbacks. If your child doesn't have a glaring difficulty, he very likely can still benefit from extra help. That's when private therapy clinics can really come to the rescue.

I'm a great proponent of ECI, because it's a program in which parents and professionals work together as a team. It is a program that provides parents with information about what they can do to help support their child's developmental needs at home. ECI therapists, for example, can help you incorporate learning opportunities into activities which are part of your child's regular routines—like meals, baths, and play time—giving you the opportunity to set developmental goals and provide therapeutic benefit to your child via those activities. They also help coordinate assistance from doctors, social services, childcare providers, and others to meet your child's specific needs.

Early intervention programs mandated by IDEA are state-funded programs that often go by a variety of names depending on the state. They provide services for children with developmental delay or disability regardless of income level. Most states use an income-based sliding scale to determine how much each family will need to pay to receive services. The first step in getting started in any state-run early-intervention program is to make a referral. This referral can come from anyone, including yourself, and can be based on anything from a family concern to a professional judgement. Just google "early childhood intervention," "ECI," or "Child Find" for programs in your area. Once that referral is made, ECI is required to perform an evaluation, typically in your home, within forty-five days. During this initial evaluation visit, the developmental specialist will use an assessment tool to identify your child's needs and determine what services your child might be eligible for.

Once eligibility is determined and your child's needs have been identified, an early-intervention team meets to develop an IFSP—an Individualized Family Service Plan. During the initial IFSP meeting, the team—which includes you, the parents—will discuss your child's current developmental benchmarks and the areas in which he needs assistance in order to grow and learn at his optimal rates and levels. Next, the team will decide what therapeutic services are needed to accomplish those goals, and how often (and where) those services will be offered—whether at home, day care, church, or another location that is specifically appropriate for your child and family. As a group, you will determine who will provide each service—a physical therapist, occupational therapist, speech therapist, or others—and carefully define goals for each type of therapy that will be offered.

ECI is excellent at providing early intervention, especially for low-income families who cannot afford private services. However, in some cases, ECI programs simply cannot replace the benefit of private services.

Private therapy services can often offer a more in-depth look at your child's developmental functioning than ECI can. When you hire a pediatric therapist privately, she or he examines the big picture and does everything possible to get your child on track. This often involves more services than are required or made possible by various ECI programs. By addressing problems that appear early, private therapists work hard to prevent larger issues from occurring down the road.

If you don't have direct access to a pediatric specialist, or you can't find anyone online, ask your pediatrician for a referral to an independent physical or occupational therapist—but be sure to seek out someone who *specializes* in pediatrics and isn't a general physical or occupational practitioner. Anyone can be trained in therapeutic techniques, but you can't easily train people how to truly relate to children. Most private therapists are more than happy to talk with you or invite you to visit their clinic before you schedule an appointment with them. You can tell a lot from these visits. Are the therapists friendly? Are they knowledgeable? Do they have a helpful office staff? Is the environment inviting? Would my child like it? The best private pediatric development practices are staffed with therapists who, first and foremost, are passionate about children and child development. They know how to relate to and motivate children, which is vitally important. This is typically something you can get a feel for fairly quickly, but only if you truly research the clinic.

Finding the Right Clinic

How do you find the therapeutic clinic that's best for your child? First, talk to friends, teachers, and other parents and search the Internet for options in your community. Then, call the clinic and ask questions. Visit its website, read the content carefully, and look at photographs of its facilities.

Even before you go for a visit, you can use your intuition to develop a "feel" for whether it's the right place for you and your child. Always remember that you are an important member of your child's therapy team and want to be able to communicate freely with your child's therapist. Therapy is not something that allows you simply to drop your kid off once or twice a week and expect him to be "fixed." Find a clinic where you can work collaboratively with your therapists, sharing concerns and new ideas, listening, brainstorming, and celebrating successes. Whenever possible, you should bring in your child's teachers and school administrators, too, making them part of the overall team. Everyone must work together for the benefit of your child, and a clinic that promotes this type of teamwork is a great asset.

Be sure to visit the clinic you're considering and take a tour. Does it look like a fun and engaging place for kids? Are the staff and therapists friendly and inviting? Is it well equipped with swings, mats, balls, and possibly even a climbing wall? Is it the kind of place where you think your child will thrive? Make sure that the therapist who will be working with your child has a degree in her field of specialty and that the clinic has a strong team of licensed physical or occupational therapists. There are clinics that offer "enrichment programs" that may seem like "therapy" but that are not staffed by licensed physical and occupational therapists. If people aren't upbeat and engaging, or ready to smile and look you in the eye, this may not be the place for you or your child. The best clinics are staffed by people who possess all the qualities that you want to see in people—*and* in your child.

Beware of clinics that only offer short, abbreviated treatments of thirty minutes or less. These programs are most often dictated by insurance requirements and not by a child's developmental needs. Children with developmental disabilities generally need a minimum of forty-five to fifty minutes of therapy time during each visit in order for it to make a significant impact on their nervous systems. I have found that thirty minutes of scheduled treatment is just never enough, especially when you account for transition and consultation time at the beginning and end of the session.

Finding a clinic that takes the time that's truly required to work with your child is critical, and when clinics are dependent on income from patients' insurance providers, problems mount, because insurance companies try hard to limit treatment times and the amount of therapy they cover. This means that many of the best clinics require direct out-of-pocket payment, leaving the filing of the actual claim to the parent.

It's not a perfect system, but we live in a society with many health insurance challenges. However, one significant advantage of direct payment is that you are able to get what you pay for without an insurance company dictating the terms. It doesn't make sense to get a professional opinion, only to have an insurance company tell you what is or is not "medically necessary." Yes, it can seem a bit overwhelming to fight the insurance-claim battles on your own, but focus on finding the right program for your child, and don't let your insurance company dictate to you what kind of treatment you can get. Ideally, make sure you decide on a clinic where your child receives consistent therapy at least once or twice a week for fifty-minute sessions or longer, one whose staff perceives you as a team member and is able to offer creative ideas for how you can help your child at home.

When you find a clinic that meets those criteria, that's at least half the battle. As soon as you, your therapy team, and your child make your initial connections, you're well on your way. The moments when you first observe a highly skilled therapist really engaging and motivating your child, seeing how excited she is to see him again, and her joy at being back in the "gym," are the times when you can be certain that you are being the greatest advocate you can be for her. Get ready to watch her fly and move beyond what she thought was possible for herself, building on her many successes along the way.

CHAPTER 5

———•———

Therapies to help build better bodies, minds, and lives . . .
   Treatments to improve your child's sensory motor development and function

Your sensory foundation affects everything you do—how you learn, how you develop both gross-motor and fine-motor skills, how you relate to those around you and modulate your behavior, how you transition from one environment to the next. As I've described, *all* of us fall somewhere on a spectrum of development that we refer to as the "sensory integration" spectrum. We each have strengths and weaknesses in the ways in which we interpret sensory information from our environment with our nervous systems. If someone has more than just a few sensory "glitches," or if the glitches are severe in any one area, those glitches can get in the way of otherwise normal development. The goal of the various therapeutic modalities used in sensory integration therapy is to pinpoint what is getting in the way of a child's "typical" development, and then help to set things right and position that child for success.

A child's "work" is play, so in order to achieve success, the child needs to be having fun, which should be easy to achieve if the child is in the right environment and can focus on activities that will strengthen his sensory foundation. Instead of bailing out a leaking boat one cup of water at a time, sensory integration therapy is about finding the "leaks" and plugging them.

Pediatric therapists are trained to engage children in new ways so they can use their nervous systems more efficiently, building strong neurological foundations for the remainder of their lives. When children can find success, they can fly, with less stress and greater joy in their lives.

Your Child's Evaluation

Once you find the right clinic, as described in the previous chapter, the next step is for your child to have a thorough sensory motor developmental evaluation. The therapist conducting this type of evaluation should be a physical or occupational therapist with a strong background in pediatrics and sensory motor development, and sensory integration. It's vital for the therapist to understand your child's strengths and weaknesses so that the most appropriate treatment plan can be prescribed. Depending on your child's age and level of function, tests will be administered and numerous clinical observations will most likely be made. Together with all the information you provide regarding your child's development to date, the therapist will develop an excellent overview of how your child perceives and interacts with the world around her, which is information that also dictates the type of therapy and therapists your child can benefit from most.

Imagine, for example, a boy in the third grade whose teacher reports that his handwriting is very messy—worrisomely so—and his mother brings him to a therapist for what she believes is a handwriting evaluation. She and her husband may have heard that occupational therapists treat handwriting issues, but at this point she may not realize that handwriting issues are almost never simply about the writing. The larger—and more fundamental question—is "What is contributing to the poor writing?" This evaluation is a very important key in unlocking these questions about what really is causing the symptoms the boy is demonstrating.

Other questions the therapist might ask could include:

- How are the boy's eyes and hands working together?
- How well developed is his bilateral coordination?
- Does he have unusual ways of moving or coordinating his body, a possible indication of the continued presence of primitive reflexes.
- Does he have trouble expressing himself verbally or in writing? Is there a difference between his proficiency levels between the two?

Think, too, about the "hyperactive" child who can't sit still in her classroom. Her teacher and parents believe she is inattentive and are worried that she has an attention deficit issue because she moves constantly and has trouble following directions and can't complete assignments that her peers are completing without problems. The therapist will try to determine what is contributing to her inattention, as well as trying to determine if she is misreading cues in her environment. (This could be followed by other questions, such as: "Is she hyper-sensitive to sounds, sights, movement, or anything else that's distracting in the background?" or "Does she have such weak core muscles that she simply can't sit still?")

Kids with inattention problems often appear to gravitate to trouble or can seem lost and unorganized. It's easy to want to focus on their behavior, but it is important to know what is setting the child up to behave this way in the first place. Let's say you have a child who tends to hit and bite her classmates instead of attending to tasks. You *can* certainly try to curb her behavior with punishment or rewards, but if the behaviors have underlying sensory motor issues, then disciplinary "tickets," "red lights," or "time-outs" are not going to fix the problem. It makes far more sense to treat the physical problem before the behavioral ones—or at least at the same time.

Following a careful evaluation, the therapist will work with the parents to develop a treatment plan aimed at developing the sensory motor foundation of that child. By addressing the individual needs of each child, more efficient neuromuscular pathways are developed—helping the brain exhibit better control over the young body.

These kinds of changes don't occur over night and there is no "quick fix." Think of the difference between a baby at birth and a six month old who is just beginning to initiate crawling motions, or the difference between a six month old who is crawling and a one-year-old child who is walking. This six-month mark becomes the benchmark for progress, and a consistency of treatment is vital for maximum progress to be made. There is a saying in neurological rehabilitation circles that "what is fired together is wired together"—and it is extremely important for us to provide kids in therapy with consistent exposure to experiences that cause these neurons to fire simultaneously so that they can ultimately become neurologically hard-wired.

Of course, no success will occur if treatment is done infrequently or for too brief a period. Steady, consistent, one-on-one therapy taking place a minimum of one or two times a week—for at least forty-five to fifty minutes per session—is critical to achieve the maximum benefit. And what goes on at home and in school to support the therapy is equally important if you hope to see big gains. By understanding what your child's sensory motor needs are, and ensuring that he gets those experiences, you are setting your child up for his greatest success.

If your child has a long way to go to catch up to his peers, the more therapy and consistency you can bring him, the better. Ideally, as I've said, forty-five to fifty-minute therapy sessions two or three times a week are the best way to begin. Once you're well under way with productive sessions and augmenting the therapy with activities at home, you may be in a position to decrease the number of weekly formal sessions, as long as they remain consistent for a minimum of six months. Twice-yearly formal re-evaluations will help gauge your child's progress with standardized measures, determining how much more therapy—if any—is needed.

Physical and Occupational Therapy

Rita, at just six months of age, was referred to us by her pediatrician when it was noticed that she didn't seem to be paying attention to the right side of her body. She had been delivered several weeks early due to low levels of fluid in utero, and now was only looking to the left.

Rita was generally a happy little girl, but completely ignored anyone who was on her right side, and she appeared to be in real danger of remaining in that condition if something did not change fairly soon.

A combination of neuromuscular and sensory integration techniques during her physical and occupational therapy allowed her to integrate both sides of her body together and "wake up" her right side, all while she engaged in play.

Rita is now in high school. Not only is she a lovely, smart young lady, she's also a beautiful dancer. Although she struggles in math, her creative writing has won high marks from her teachers. Her right-sided movement is entirely normal and equal to the left; and she is lithe, coordinated, and athletic.

Physical and occupational therapists are the providers of the treatment we refer to as sensory integration therapy—meaning therapy which utilizes a variety of treatment techniques that embrace the theory and treatment philosophy of Dr. A. Jean Ayres, about whom I wrote earlier. As an occupational therapist and educational psychologist, Ayres was an expert in her field and contributed significantly to the treatment of children with learning differences.

The distinctions between physical and occupational therapists can be confusing, especially in the world of pediatrics. Simply stated, physical therapy is typically focused on helping children improve their gross-motor skills, coordination, strength, and gait; while occupational therapy for children is typically aimed at helping them increase their fine-motor skills, handwriting, academic performance, and social skills. However, *both* kinds of therapy directly enhance sensory integration, behavior, the development of motor skills overall (gross *and* fine motor), academic success, and greater self-confidence.

Children with developmental delays and disabilities, cerebral palsy, or genetic disorders, or who have suffered accidents or sports injuries, are often referred to a physical therapist, first. Occupational therapists, on the other hand, see more patients who have learning differences, cognitive planning challenges, self-care issues, and behavioral, social, and emotional health concerns. However, both specialties offer valuable input into the successful treatment of sensory integration deficits, autism spectrum disorders, developmental delays, and musculo-skeletal problems, as well as helping to restore an individual to a previous level of function if an accident or injury had occurred.

For instance, as a physical therapist, I am trained in kinesiology, anatomy, physiology, and neurology. The focus of most physical therapists is the body's muscles and the neurology that allows our muscles and whole bodies to move and function in specific ways. In pediatrics, physical therapists specifically deal with the physical child and how the child moves, grows, and develops. We focus on our young patients' entire developmental profile and always attempt to be attuned to the child's and family's needs at the same time.

Occupational therapists typically concentrate their professional energies on their patients' functional activities, including dressing, school performance, behavior, handwriting, and social skills. Neither field ignores one area at the expense of another. We treat the whole child, bringing together our individual areas of specialization in combination with sensory integration techniques that include vestibular, proprioceptive, and tactile input. It's ideal to work with a team of therapists who can work together for the benefit of both the child and family, getting the best of both worlds and the combined intelligence that exceeds any one profession.

For example, if we've determined that a child needs twice-a-week therapy, ideally I prefer that the child work with a physical therapist during one session and an occupational therapist the next—not because the therapies are dramatically different, but simply because the two therapists are inevitably going to perceive and work with the young patient a bit differently based on their backgrounds (and that's a good thing). The two therapists will be able to share their impressions with each other, as well as with the parents, helping to address the child's needs and progress in a more comprehensive manner.

These days, therapists in general tend to be seeing more children with torticollis (abnormal tilting or twisting of the head and neck) as well as plagiocephaly (abnormal shaping of the head). As we have discussed previously, both of these occur, in part, because of the successful implementation of the "back to sleep" program, which is aimed at reducing the incidence of SIDS by ensuring that infants sleep on their backs. Unfortunately, when newborns spend the majority of their time in only one position, their necks can tighten asymmetrically, and their heads can mold in unusual patterns. In extreme cases, a child may begin to look solely to one side and to ignore looking to the other side of his body completely (as happened in Rita's case, above).

Traditionally, in this type of case, physical therapists will address the range of motion in the infant's neck, using stretches and other exercises to get the neck to begin to move bilaterally and equally. The focus tends to be on the muscles and the child's range of motion, so the child can more easily eat and can look to both sides equally as a result.

An occupational therapist, on the other hand, may be more focused on the act of feeding, working to make sure the baby can nurse successfully at both breasts, for example, and can turn and roll in both directions in order to reach and play with a toy. The emphasis of each of the two treatments is different, but the goals are ultimately the same. No matter what the professional background of the therapist is, the attention is focused on the obstacles that are currently in the way of the child's normal development—and how they can be overcome.

We also see many young patients who have had repetitive ear infections as infants. These can be caused by a number of different factors related to the Eustachian tubes not draining effectively in the ears. These issues can set a child up not only for speech and language issues, but can also affect the child's balance and coordination. If a child's vestibular system is compromised, whether from frequent ear infections or a difficult delivery, balance and coordination, as well as strength and motor planning, can suffer. The impacts of these conditions can be subtle or severe, but it is not uncommon for this early childhood issue to become a significant developmental issue later.

It's vital for parents to have their kids' ear infections treated, but looking at the cause of the infection is equally important. If your daughter is having a lot of ear infections, what's the reason? And what can we do to help prevent them? Is her diet a factor? Are her Eustachian tubes misshapen or in an unusual position? Does she have constant allergies, swelling, or congestion that is preventing her tubes from draining? It's not uncommon to forget about these early problems, especially when they don't seem to be major ones at the time. However, a year or two later, some of your daughter's inability to sit still, inattention, or auditory processing challenges may actually be related to those early ear infections and will be an important part of her medical history when you and your therapists are trying to sort out how best to help her.

I can't tell you how many times I've encountered a child whose parents have been told that he has attention deficit disorder, but who, on evaluation, truly exhibits an imbalance of musculature, which makes it next to impossible for him to sit still. So, he wiggles around constantly, unless he's deep in a beanbag chair or propped up with his arms on a tabletop to help hold himself steady. The therapeutic treatment for muscular imbalance or weakness is dramatically different than treating a brain with medications. Pediatric physical and occupational therapy focus on strengthening, balancing, and coordinating the body so the child has the motor control to sit still. When that happens, it's amazing the impact it can have on inattention.

Therapists, Side by Side

In a therapy clinic in which physical and occupational therapists work side by side, standardized testing and structured clinical observations are commonplace. Patterns of how a child interacts with his environment and with other children offer important clues as to how her underlying sensory systems are working.

For instance, the ways in which a child responds to movement and changes in her body position can be directly related to how she can interact with others and pay attention. Therapists will watch her eyes closely for their reaction to spinning or swinging. Do they flicker back and forth, or are they still? How dizzy does she get or does she not respond at all? Does the spinning make her feel sick to her stomach or does it make her want to run around the room crashing into everything in sight immediately afterwards? These are all important clues into how the vestibular system is processing movement information and may be affecting behavior and functional performance.

The physical therapist and occupational therapist treating the child each see things through their own professional eyes and experience—which is the best possible situation for questioning parents. As therapists make note of how your child is adjusting to movement experiences, they will provide her with different activities aimed at integrating this information more appropriately, They will watch for how she organizes her body in order to play with others and will always work to motivate her to create her own "just right" activities rather than simply responding to commands—which is something very different from what tends to happen in physical education classes or organized sports.

The therapists' goal is focused on encouraging your child to challenge her body in new and different ways and build on her success, tapping into her internal drive to do more. When this happens, we know things are moving in the right direction and that there are no limits to how far she can go. It is much more than simply what happens in the gym or under the watchful eye of the therapist. It has to do with the internal spark that suddenly flares and allows your child to gather more of these appropriate experiences on her own, creating new and vital neural pathways.

In the first couple of sessions, your therapist will plan most of what takes place. For example, he might set up a series of swings and objects and suggest, "Let's try to move from this swing to this block to this pillow." The activity is designed so that the child is met with success, no matter how timid or impulsive. The young patient responds, has fun, feels successful—sometimes for the first time—and begins to get to know the equipment and trust the environment. The child discovers that swings and activities have unusual names that help tap into their imaginations and add to the fun—new names such as "frog swings," "moon swings," and "bolster swings," "bolder dash," "scooter-board hockey," and "crash-in-the-cake"—in combination with all sorts of blocks, pillows, and slides that form ever-evolving obstacle courses.

Over time, the therapist will solicit the help of the child in creating her own "obstacle course," asking "What should we do next? What combination sounds fun to you?" Nonverbal children use pictures to help organize their thoughts and communicate their wishes, and it's amazing what the kids can come up with on their own. Not only will a good therapist work to keep children engaged and having a good time, but also to push them beyond what they currently can do on their own, always building on their successes and never making things so challenging that they give up—or so easy that they get bored.

We find that, many times, children begin to seek out the kinds of activities that their bodies need to master, or activities that can help them improve. When the ideas come from the children, not only are they vested in them, but they are all the more proud when they have successfully challenged themselves and "won," which inevitably leads to greater triumphs.

We also work with parents on this concept. For example, it is not uncommon for dads to get out and "play ball" with their sons—but sometimes those dads do it a little too enthusiastically. After only two or three balls are thrown too hard or from too far away, the kids can quickly decide that the game is over. Yet, when the dad starts out with easy tasks, such as tossing a pillow from just a few feet away, it's amazing how much more engaged the child can become. Then, over time, they can gradually increase the difficulty level of their games.

When a child experiences trust and success, he is much more likely to want to do more and both parent (or therapist) and child are likely to experience a much more enjoyable interaction.

The Healing Therapy of Gentle Touch

The first time I treated Jeffrey, he was paralyzed with fear, but a combination of sensory integration therapy and CranioSacral Therapy (CST) proved to be perfect for him.

The CST—a gentle, non-invasive, manual therapy technique—caused his cheeks to grow bright red and he fell sound asleep during our first session. His anxiety was absent when he awoke and his parents couldn't believe how calm he appeared. He began to try new things, not just in the gym, but also at home, and his confidence grew.

We treated Jeffrey throughout his school years with regular CST and sensory integration therapy. When he reached high school, he would come in for periodic "tune-ups" and would still fall asleep on my table, the therapy taking the edge off his high-anxiety nature for the months that followed.

Today, Jeffrey is in his early twenties. He has a girlfriend and a job, and his parents (who never thought they would see this day), wonder why he doesn't call home more often—just like every other parent of a college kid. He's on his way to a happy, engaging, and independent life.

Physical and occupational therapies tend to be all about movement, but the benefits of the CST include a profound relaxation response, along with improved functioning of the individual. CST is frequently used to relieve pain, tension, and body dysfunction—as well as to improve sensory function, motor coordination, developmental progress, neuromuscular function, and overall health. This system involves the structures of the central nervous system (the brain, the spinal cord, and the peripheral nervous system), the bones that surround it (the cranial bones, spine, and tailbone), the fluid that is circulated within in (the cerebrospinal fluid), and the connective tissue throughout our body.

This gentle, and yet highly effective, modality was developed by Dr. John E. Upledger, beginning in the 1970s. As a highly innovative osteopathic physician, Dr. Upledger demonstrated extensive clinical successes and pioneered research at Michigan State University and the

Upledger Institute in Florida over the course of four decades. Since its inception, over 100,000 practitioners have been trained worldwide, and CST's benefits continue to be documented—and are confirmed every day by the patients who have received this treatment from skilled practitioners.

Certainly controversial in its early years of use, CST has found its way into mainstream medicine as more and more physicians, therapists, and patients around the world have experienced it first hand—and have recommended it to others. CranioSacral therapists are trained to identify and treat subtle characteristics within the CranioSacral system, noting changes in the cerebrospinal fluid's rhythm, rate, amplitude, and quality as they gently work with their patients' heads and body tissues. As a therapist works with a patient, he applies his hands gently onto the body using only about five grams of pressure over the body's natural resistance (about the weight of an American nickel). This allows for a significant relaxation response throughout the body as the tissues soften under the touch. To get a sense of how subtle this touch is, you might imagine holding onto a full balloon with two hands while someone sticks a finger into the side of your balloon. The gentle increase in resistance that you should feel is what the therapist might detect under his hands while working with a person. What makes this an even more ideal treatment, especially for children, is that it can be done in any treatment space—whether the client is lying quietly on a massage table, sitting on a platform swing while being gently rocked, or playing with toys on the floor. This extremely relaxing treatment can yield lasting results with no negative side effects, and—for children—it can open the way for greater gains and success in a variety of physical and neurological functions over a shorter period of time.

Both physical and occupational therapists are accustomed to action, and to getting muscles to respond in a certain, predictable way. As a physical therapist, I had been trained to tap, stretch, rub, and massage muscles in an effort to get them to respond the way I wanted or expected them to. It was easy to understand that bodies needed to move to develop strength and balance, and this very light touch seemed counter-intuitive at first—but I was in for a surprise. Training to become a CranioSacral therapist involves the opposite. The practitioner is taught how to take the pressure *off* the body—rather than actively stimulating the muscles—and to gently allow the soft tissues under the hands to simply relax. Patients often express a deep relaxation response as a result, with a resurgence of energy that follows.

When Jeffrey received his first treatment on a long platform swing, with my hands initially gently held over the front and back of his body, I waited for him to relax under my touch. Soon I could feel his body warm up and soften. This change was a signal that I could move my hands slowly to the next place on his body where the same thing occurred again. By the end of our session, fifty minutes later, he was asleep in my arms, and I carried him out to the waiting room. He woke up with rosy cheeks and gave his mother a big hug.

The next day, the boy's mother called to report to me that he had sat at the dinner table for the first time ever and had eaten his entire meal—and that she wanted to schedule another treatment as soon as she could get him in. Soon, his language began to emerge at a rapid pace, and he accelerated in his therapeutic progress. I was hooked—and so were his parents.

A Wonderful Adjunct to All Other Therapies

Discovering a therapeutic modality that could initiate such big changes in a very short amount of time was completely new to me eighteen years ago. As we all know, therapy simply takes time, and we all recognize that there are no quick fixes. Yet, when I began to observe the dramatic changes in so many kids after just a few CranioSacral sessions, I knew this was something we needed to do more of with the children we were treating.

The more I learned, the less I realized I knew—which is a circumstance that continues to motivate progressive therapists to keep an open mind and grow professionally. I truly believe that practitioners do a disservice to their patients if they stop seeking answers and only offer them the status quo that they are familiar with. No matter how "outside the box" something may seem at first, there are many new treatment styles that warrant exploration. Thinking and investigating beyond the walls of the mainstream scientific-method box makes great sense when you realize that everyone really is different. This realization, in turn, makes it impossible to dismiss out of hand many of these innovative treatments. In my case, I'm grateful that I was open to discovering what CranioSacral Therapy could offer to our clients.

I met Brent, when he was six months old, following a life-threatening bout of bacterial meningitis. His parents, both physicians, felt strangely out of control, and were understandably extremely worried parents. Brent had begun to suffer from near-constant seizures—sometimes several per minute—requiring increasing doses of anti-seizure medications.

Brent's parents clearly understood the statistical possibility that the meningitis and constant seizures could result in permanent disability, and the CranioSacral Therapy that we recommended seemed a little far-fetched to them at first, but they decided that, if it could help, they were willing to try it. It certainly didn't seem like it could hurt him, compared to everything else he was going through.

Gradually, over the course of the next two years, while continuing to receive weekly CST, he was able to be slowly weaned off his seizure medication under his neurologist's care, and to remain seizure free.

Today, he is a talented musician attending college, his precarious beginning far behind him. His story is a great example of how mainstream and complementary medicine can come together for the overall good of a patient.

Another example of this teamwork between medical specialists occurred in the case of the formerly conjoined Egyptian twins, Ahmed and Mohamed Ibrahim. CranioSacral Therapy played an important role in preparing the twins for their world-renowned separation surgery in October 2003—performed in Dallas by a team of fifty physicians and led by Dr. Kenneth Salyer, one of the world's foremost reconstructive plastic surgeons. Several CranioSacral therapists were part of that team, and it was our job to work with the two boys, who were joined at the top of their skulls, to prepare their bodies and internal systems for a surgery that would be enormously physically challenging for them— even if everything went according to plan. This was a new challenge for all of us. Not only did we have a complicated medical case to deal with, but we also had to deal with two separate cranial systems that were attached in the middle.

When the boys first came to us, they were carried by two nurses, who held them as if they were a log, with their shared skull in the middle of two bodies that extended in opposite directions. Initially, the boys were extremely sensitive to movement, and when one moved, the other was instantly affected—often in a way the other did not like—and the movement that *was* possible was obviously very limited. For a year, we worked with them several times each week to help the boys gain weight, strength, and muscle tone, and even to learn how to eat and walk. Several of us would hold one boy upside down as the other gained experience standing on his own two legs. Little by little, their tolerance to this activity improved and they were able to take their first steps, preparing each for walking independently after their surgery. There were no books or manuals to guide us, and the challenge required a great deal of thinking outside the box. Physical and occupational therapy were vital parts of our overall regimen along with the CST, which helped their autonomic nervous systems to relax and be more receptive to all the other therapeutic input, boosting their physical gains.

Dr. Upledger, himself, came to Dallas to be part of the CranioSacral team and we were able to take the boys to the Upledger Institute in Florida, as well. The children thrived, and by the time the separation surgery—which lasted thirty-three hours—was finally performed, they were ready. The surgery was an overwhelming success in the end. Like everyone on our very large team, we were all delighted by what we had collectively accomplished.

Dr. Salyer, the twins, and the story of their successful separation surgery and treatment were all featured on numerous shows including *Dateline* and *The Oprah Winfrey Show*, as well as on *The Discovery Channel*, receiving media attention from around the world. It was an extraordinary experience, and also a wonderful opportunity to demonstrate what an invaluable complementary tool CranioSacral Therapy can be, even in the most extreme situations.

Today the twins are happy thirteen year olds, living in their two separate, healthy bodies with their family in Egypt.

Training the Brain

Ryan was a fifteen-year-old boy who had been struggling to keep up with increasing homework demands in his sophomore year of high school. He liked sports, but his grades were sliding downwards and he was fearful of being placed on academic probation.

As a result, he was becoming increasingly anxious, frustrated, and depressed. His parents, appropriately concerned, had heard about the Interactive Metronome (IM) program from a friend and decided to give it a try.

At first, Ryan was resistant, thinking that admitting he was in trouble somehow meant he wasn't "good enough." Fortunately, he decided to give it a try after hearing about some professional athletes who had used it to improve their sports performance.

After a couple of sessions with an enthusiastic IM trainer, Ryan was hooked. He began to look forward to the sessions, proving to himself each time that he could do it, as he improved his scores with each increasing challenge. As a result, his grades (and his sport performance) began to improve.

After just fifteen sessions, he was back on track. His anxiety and frustration had decreased and he was feeling better about himself once again.

Ryan still comes in for periodic tune-ups over the holidays, to keep that success going. In addition, his parents invested in IM-Home®, the home version, which is designed to provide an avenue for additional practice.

Using the metronome as a tool has been utilized for decades in a variety of disciplines. In the early 1990s, acoustical engineer Jim Cassilly developed the Interactive Metronome (IM), originally to help professional musicians improve productivity and outcomes in the recording studio. In addition to his work in the studio, he also taught piano lessons to autistic children at a private school. A pilot study using the Interactive Metronome as part of these children's treatment plan yielded significant improvements and caught the attention of child psychiatrist Dr. Stanley Greenspan. (Dr. Greenspan, best known for his development of the "Floortime Approach," and for numerous books involving the treatment of children with developmental disabilities and autistic spectrum disorders, later became the director of the Interactive Metronome's Scientific Advisory Board.) A variety of studies have since followed, proving multiple benefits in using this tool for everything from athletics to learning and behavior.

The science behind IM involves the actual timing of the brain, which has been found to be linked with a variety of diagnoses including ADHD, dyslexia, autism, auditory processing disorder, Parkinson's disease, and schizophrenia, as well as in other learning differences affecting reading and writing. Brain research has demonstrated that several regions of the brain must be in sync for the brain and body to perform efficiently. Networks of nerves must turn on and off, sending signals at precisely the right time in order to get the job done. If some parts of this complex network take too long or don't communicate with the other parts effectively, the result is difficulty in performing the task, whether it is in paying attention, processing what is being said, speaking, controlling behavior, or coordinating movements. When this timing in the brain and body is addressed, coupled with fun, functional, whole-body motor activities, significant treatment outcomes can be accomplished. We now know that synchronized timing in the brain is critical for a whole host of abilities including speech, language, auditory processing, visual processing, reading, writing, attention, cognitive speed, working memory, executive functions, motor skills, coordination, balance, sensory processing, and more.

In a study published in the *American Journal of Occupational Therapy* (Robert J. Shaffer, et al., 2000), five areas of statistically significant improvement impacted by Interactive Metronome therapy were identified. These improvements were in the areas of attention and focus, motor control and coordination, language processing, reading and math fluency, and the ability to regulate aggression and impulsivity.

IM is now one of the most widely used programs in the world for cognitive development and rehabilitation, no matter what the cognitive or physical challenge. Twelve to fifteen sessions can be effective for many, while others with more processing and motor impairment may require a longer, and more stepwise, approach to the training. Either way, the use of this tool can make a huge difference in how a student or athlete can perform in school or on the field.

I've been a huge proponent of IM for many years, and have a great deal of first-hand experience with what it can accomplish for children and adults experiencing a wide array of issues and challenges. Recent IM technology uses a game-like auditory-visual computer platform that is fun for the kids and is able to provide constant feedback to the millisecond while performing customized programs designed to meet the individualized needs of each child. The differences between the patient's response time and the actual beats are measured and scored, and the child works progressively to lower his scores. Over a period of four to five weeks, this invariably leads to improved performance of many kinds, whether with attention, cognition, focus, or coordination issues. This also contributes to the synchronized timing in the brain, which is critical for executive functioning. While I am typically not a huge fan of computer games for children (as I have already mentioned), this is one instance where I do think this platform is worthwhile. The difference is that the child working with IM is actively participating with his whole body, while interacting with the therapist and building on success.

IM is great for strengthening attention and focus, and its repetitive nature helps nerves to fire together in a way that they weren't asked to do before. By repeatedly attempting novel movement and body positions until, at last, the patient gets them right, leading to new patterns and neural connections.

For a child who has problems focusing in school, IM can be of great help, as well. In a typical therapy session, the child arrives at his IM session, places headphones on his ears, then plays a game that involves hitting a trigger with his hands or feet at the precise moment he hears a cowbell tone—one that recurs in precise patterns. Kids of all ages—and adults, too—find it fun and consistently challenging. Individuals who typically find it hard to slow down and focus almost always start out responding ahead of the actual beat rather than behind it. But, with time and practice, the child learns not only to precisely match the beat but will also see his behavior in school change as focusing and slowing his movements becomes easier and more automatic.

Multi-Sensory Listening Therapy

Dawn was three when I first met her. She had a thick shock of sandy hair and bright blue eyes, but she screamed in protest at any change or new face. Consequently, she had a hard time attending school and seemed lost and frustrated in her own world.

Early on, her parents, both busy attorneys, had been proactive in enrolling her into a language-based preschool program, but by the age of three, her language, social, and motor skills still lagged far behind those of her peers. When she first started physical and occupational therapy, she was not only extremely anxious, but also stiff and rigid, as if she did not know what to do with her body. When someone tossed a ball in her direction, her hands stayed at her sides. In a game of patty-cake, she quickly fell out of rhythm and lost interest.

While we worked with her in the clinic to strengthen and integrate her body more effectively, the Integrated Listening System (iLs) was recommended as a home program, to additionally facilitate her speech and motor centers together.

Dawn is now six years old and attends a Dallas-area school that does a fabulous job of serving children who learn differently. Not only is she enrolled in a school that utilizes progressive teaching techniques, motivating and empowering children's bright, young, yet often-misunderstood minds, but teachers also recognize the need for early intervention therapy. We are very fortunate to have a clinic and therapeutic gym on campus, so

Dawn is able to receive therapy during the school day without having to leave the campus, as well as continuing to use her iLs at home.

After just a year and a half of therapy, Dawn is happy, thriving, and has become a very verbal child—a far cry from the quiet, stiff child I first met. She carries on normal conversations, has appropriate motor skills, and loves her friends and school. I suspect no one will imagine she had early hurdles to overcome by the time she's an adult.

Integrated Listening Systems (iLs) is a new type of sound therapy (also called "listening therapy") which builds on techniques originally developed in France decades ago. While most listening therapies focus on stimulation of the auditory system, iLs trains the brain and body to process multi-sensory information by combining auditory, vestibular, visual, and balance activities into a single program. Today, iLs, together with a variety of other listening-based programs, is used with great success in sensory development clinics around the world.

Therapists appreciate iLs as an adjunct to therapy because of its multi-sensory input and convenience of use as a home program. Like the Interactive Metronome, it is capable of "re-wiring" areas of the brain which are involved with learning, communication, emotional regulation, and movement. University research and clinical data have demonstrated that children who receive iLs therapy demonstrate significant improvement in auditory processing, memory, attention, and behavior. School data similarly reveals that students can improve their reading skills by an average of two years with just three months of therapy, even if they are already on track—it's pretty remarkable.

As I described back in chapter two, the body's visual, auditory, and vestibular systems are responsible for understanding and organizing sensory input. iLs therapy exercises all three of those systems in a staged program which becomes progressively more challenging from one session to the next. A child working with iLs wears special headphones attached to an MP3 player and mini-amp, which are worn in a waist pack. The headphones are unique in that they replicate how we hear ourselves when we speak, i.e. through both air and bone (every time we speak, the sound travels by air to our outer ear, as well as through the vibration of the larynx which is carried internally, by bone, to the inner ear). The iLs headphones mimic this by sending music through the ear cup and also through a transducer fitted to the inside top of the headphones. As a result, the auditory and vestibular systems are trained to work together. Through exercises which combine iLs with visual and balance exercises on a repeated basis, the child gradually learns to process *simultaneous* multi-sensory input. This has the effect of making a child more functionally competent, which in turn increases her self-confidence. With increased confidence, her social skills and behavior will improve; those children suffering from anxiety or insecurity often begin to exhibit a sunnier disposition and a new attitude toward life. In this way, we often see a kind of transformation occur, starting with a mix of symptoms related to an inability to process information and ending with a self-confident and balanced child.

An important aspect of iLs programs is that they are customizable: one program targets sensory processing, another attention and focus, another language and communication. One of the things I particularly like about iLs is that it takes "listening therapy" to a higher level by addressing brain fitness in a global way. The programs progress in a very gentle way to avoid over-stimulating those children with hypersensitivities, and yet they are designed so that the therapist can effectively target specific issues for different clients' needs.

The integration of movement with the sound component is key: by improving a child's ability to sense where her own body is in space, and how to control and move it, her brain is freed to focus on higher-order activities. She becomes able to approach learning and communication tasks in a more relaxed and regulated manner, improving her attention, becoming calmer, and gaining coordination and confidence.

In computer terms, our cerebellum is our brain's processor, receiving input from our sensory systems and various parts of the brain, and integrating these inputs to regulate and fine-tune motor activity. Repetitive iLs exercises stimulate function in the cerebellum, training it to become more efficient at processing multi-sensory information. In my experience, iLs can offer great help in stimulating connections between the right and left hemispheres of the brain via the corpus callosum, as well. Its combination of listening and physical exercises, using both sides of the body together, demand the constant transfer of information from one side of the brain to the other, strengthening existing pathways and building new ones.

For the younger child who is resistant to headphones, a special pillow called the "Dreampad" was developed by iLs. This consists of a pillow which has the same technology as the iLs headphones (bone conduction transducers) embedded in it. The Dreampad plays music from an app which one downloads to a smart phone (or to an MP3 player). The music has been processed to emphasize frequencies which facilitate sleep, i.e. a slow tempo and no melodies which would be overly engaging for the brain. The result is music, and a method of delivering it, which brings about a relaxation response in the nervous system. It can easily be used to help children calm down and transition into sleep while preparing them for better listening at the same time.

A Therapeutic Team

I'm committed to the notion that kids with developmental challenges benefit most when they have the option of being treated with multiple therapeutic modalities by multiple specialists. Everyone is different and there is not one right way to treat all kids. As fundamental as physical and occupational therapy are to helping children overcome sensory integration issues, other complementary therapies that are often used in conjunction with physical and occupational therapy, such as Interactive Metronome, Integrative Listening Systems, and CranioSacral Therapy, also provide vital help in yielding better and faster results.

During my decades of practice, I've never been one to quickly embrace the therapeutic modality of the moment. I need to investigate, then to see real results with my patients before I can endorse a particular therapeutic technique. Those I've outlined in this chapter are the therapies I know, believe in, and have employed with great success with a multitude of young patients.

I'm also someone who is deeply committed to treating children with teams of therapists whenever possible. When professionals with diverse backgrounds and differing perspectives come together to solve a difficult puzzle, great things happen. Kids with developmental delays seldom have only a single issue. We rarely see only a physical therapy problem such as torticollis or club feet; we rarely see just an occupational issue like poor handwriting or trouble getting organized for school; and a picky eater is seldom simply a picky eater. When multiple therapists are focused on the patterns of needs of a particular child, it's far more likely that the root problem can be discovered, then successfully addressed, before seemingly minor issues develop into bigger problems.

Those of us who are blessed to be in the business of helping kids fly are like the mechanics who work in teams to ensure that great airliners can safely leave the ground and transport their passengers to destinations around the globe. We don't strive to be in the limelight, but we know that we do critically important work. Kids are *meant* to fly, and we can all help ensure that they do.

CHAPTER 6

———•———

What comes next?
The journey ahead

Young patients and parents alike tend to report with excitement that "things are better" soon after sensory integration therapy begins and well before enough time has passed for true neurological change to have occurred. Kids simply feel happier with themselves as they try new things; activities are suddenly easier for them, and their parents often note corresponding behavioral changes that assure them they have made an excellent decision for their child's future.

In therapy, we often see improvements from one session to the next. Goals are adjusted as they are met and the success continues to build. Therapy is never a quick fix, although change sometimes comes at a rapid pace, especially when there is a consistent, comprehensive program in place and the parents are contributing with sensory-motor activities at home. Each child's motivation is also a key factor in progress, and it's one we are always focused on.

Parents play a critical role in providing feedback to their children's therapists. We want (and need) to know what is going on at home and at school. You know your child better than anyone, and giving therapists as much feedback as you can allows us to work with you to solve problems, creating faster solutions. If a boy is struggling with his letters in school, his therapist needs to know about it. She's a developmental specialist armed with a toolbox full of experience that can be very helpful, but she won't know what tools to use if she doesn't know what is in need of improvement.

Therapy normally requires a significant stretch of time simply because nerves grow slowly, and a therapist's work is aimed at facilitating that growth process by stimulating neural pathways in new ways. This, in turn, helps the nerves find connections in a fraction of the time they would need without therapeutic assistance. It's a bit like the time it takes for a transplanted tree to spread its roots out into the surrounding soil and become stable—or like a tree slowly sending new branches upward to reach the light. That growth is essential for a strong, healthy tree—*and* it requires patience.

Because of the time it takes for change to happen, therapists can't confirm any vital neurological changes until consistent therapy has taken place for at least six months and re-testing is done. Standardized testing is typically done every six to eight months, to demonstrate the benefit of the therapy and because insurance companies (along with parents) want empirical proof of the value of their expenditures—both of money and time.

The most important reason for testing, however, is to determine how quickly the child is changing over a given six- to eight-month period. Is she approaching the world differently and more accurately? Is he boldly trying new things on his own? Has she become happier since the therapy began? Is he growing into his body? The answers to those questions are just as important as any standardized markers of progress. Our ultimate goal—that of the therapists, the parents, and the teachers—is to help each child to become able to make the most of her body, her mind, and her spirit—and to help her grow into a happy and productive adult. It's the goal we all strive for, and it's one that allows those of us who love our work to view this work as a privilege.

The standardized results at each re-evaluation are compared with the initial evaluation scores from six or eight months earlier, and we are never surprised when a developmental gap has closed much more quickly than even we would expect. This is a great sign, in fact, because not only does it confirm the benefits of the therapy, but it also gives us a great picture of what is really going on with each child.

During therapy, it is not uncommon to see eight, twelve, or even fifteen months' worth of developmental gain in just six months of time. When scores close quickly, we know that the nervous system is changing and developing in the right direction, suggesting that the child has a straightforward, mild sensory processing disorder. When scores close more slowly, they suggest that there may be a bigger issue going on and we may want to increase the number of therapy sessions a child has each week, or add new techniques. There are a variety of different means with which we can evaluate progress along the way, but we are always most interested in change that's taking place at home and at school—which, after all, is really what's most important. The standardized scores simply give us a predictable benchmark to measure against, while the "real-world" change is the true goal.

These scores also give important feedback to your child's physician, so he can more accurately diagnose what may be at the root of a problem. Slower gains tend to predict years in treatment, while with faster gains the length of treatment is typically between six months and two years. How quickly your child changes is often the most reliable predictor of his ultimate functional capabilities and diagnoses. I have worked with children, for example, who initially appeared to have some significant autistic characteristics, yet with treatment ended up being highly functional over a relatively short period of time. No matter how fast or how slow, we are always striving to close that developmental gap, paving the way for greater success

Ending Things Too Soon
It doesn't happen often, but sometimes a child's therapy is stopped

just when great progress is beginning to be made. At times, insurance companies refuse to continue paying for therapy; occasionally parents become impatient; and sometimes parents simply think their child has begun to do "good enough." But it's a big risk for a child to find a groove and really begin to put his sensory challenges behind him, only to stop before he's entirely there—before true neurological change is complete.

When you create momentum, facilitate positive changes, and demonstrate to a child that she *can* do many things she long believed she couldn't—and then stop that support and training—the experience can be very troubling. New self-confidence can retreat; old patterns can re-emerge, and the child can slip back into a world filled with new frustrations. Over time, the parents often begin to see the developmental gap widen again as their child gets older, yet is unable to keep up with the progress she was making before. If the foundation for progress is not fully in place as she gets older, she often does not have the tools to keep up with her chronological age, and holes in her skills will begin to emerge again.

It is critical that, no matter when or why a child takes a break from therapy, he continue with a strong "sensory diet"—not the diet of what he eats, but the "diet" of activities he undertakes. Think about what happens to you and your body when you stop working out: you lose both strength and endurance. The same thing happens to children when therapy is ended too early or isn't followed with consistent exercise, which results in limiting their bodies' abilities to sustain the continued neural growth necessary for steady improvement.

We want your child to build a strong foundation—and to take flight from that foundation—flying in self-confidence, with pride in their accomplishments. Our hearts soar when we see that they're getting it all together—they're moving well; they feel good about themselves; they are enjoying the challenges they face; and they love it when they surmount those hurdles.

There are other situations in which it's clearly time to begin cutting the amount of therapy back—not ending it suddenly, but beginning to transition toward the time when it will stop. Every child is different, but sometimes it makes sense to take a break from therapy, or to decrease the number of treatment sessions. Good therapists have an uncanny way of knowing when it makes sense to cut back and how to go about it, so talk to your therapists and work on scheduling with them so your child can get the full advantage of what therapy has to offer.

Keep in mind that children who have significant developmental disabilities are less likely to keep the momentum going during big breaks. You will notice this change in momentum in their deteriorating behavior, and you'll be very happy to get them back to therapy as soon as you can. These are the kids who will likely need ongoing therapy for years in order to keep their momentum going. But, for kids who are successfully overcoming sensory integration delays and other minor issues, breaks from therapy and the planned tapering down of the amount of therapy often make good sense as their parents and therapists collectively decide on the best next steps.

Something that's important to remember in this regard is that we have a large—yet finite—window of opportunity to make significant developmental changes before a child reaches adolescence. Once puberty begins and hormones begin to kick in, it becomes much more challenging to interact with, engage, and motivate kids like we can do successfully earlier on. We can accomplish great things with sensory integration therapy for the first ten to twelve years of a child's life. But, if the work begins too late—or if it ends too early—future results may not be as dramatic as they could otherwise have been.

Don't Try to Be Your Child's Therapist

As parents, we all feel we know what's best for our children. That's our job; no one is as vitally invested with love and concern for our children as we are. It simply goes without saying. We believe we know our kids the best and we *do*, yet it is impossible to be both your child's parent *and* your child's therapist. You are your child's safety net, and no matter how hard you try—or how experienced you are—because you are able to interpret his every move and emotion, finding that "just-right challenge" for your child is next to impossible.

When I finally realized my son, Alex, needed therapy, I knew I couldn't be his therapist. It wasn't because I didn't have the skills, but because I saw him differently—he was my son. I would have driven him crazy, and he would have frustrated me to no end, despite the fact that we clearly had a close and loving relationship. I simply could not have gotten the same amount of effort from him that his therapist did. He inevitably tried harder and did more for her than he would have for me, because Alex and I both knew how to unconsciously predict each other's responses—and unfortunately how to push each other's buttons, as well.

You have an incredibly important relationship with your child; you are his parent, and it's a relationship that will never end. But you are not his best friend, nor are you his instructor. Yes, he learns a great deal from you—from your modeling and from your behavior. But that doesn't mean you would be the perfect person to teach him math, or to help him work through bigger developmental issues.

The goal in sensory integration therapy is to motivate kids to go well beyond what they would otherwise attempt and accomplish on their own, building on their successes along the way. And, precisely because you know your daughter so well, it's all too easy for you to unconsciously anticipate what *you* believe she can do or will attempt to try. Because you've never seen her scale a climbing wall, for example— or show the slightest bit of interest in climbing—you may well assume that climbing might hold no interest for her. Despite your very best intentions, your perceptions may actually get in the way of her experiencing this new challenge, even though that activity may be just the thing to kick-start her development.

The activities we use in therapy are simple and creative forms of play. However, we are constantly watching for the desired responses and outcomes to build on. For those of us who undertake this work professionally, and who do it well, we have had years of formal training, followed with even more clinical experience. (Who knew that play could be so complicated?) We've learned *how* to motivate kids to do things differently, *how* to read the signs and signals of their neurological thresholds, and *how* to push them beyond their comfort zones as we build on their new successes. We've got to be endlessly creative and acutely observant—able to see the difference, for example, between fear and a physical inability to accomplish a new task, to differentiate between neurological responses and changes in mood or levels of stress.

The best kinds of therapists are constantly working to get inside each child, so to speak—into their nervous systems and into their brains where the real therapeutic changes are taking place. Therapists may well have to alter their treatment techniques four or five times during a single, hour-long session, depending on what kind of day the child is having and what kind of responses the child is giving in that moment. Therapists build trust, confidence, self-esteem—and friendship—in the context of a relationship that nonetheless remains professional in the very best way.

Be a Partner—and Cheerlead a Little, Too!

By far the best role you can play during your child's therapy is to be a partner in the process—joining your daughter in her enthusiasm for her weekly trips to the "gym," following up on the therapist's suggestions for complementary exercises you and she can do at home, and celebrating her successes as they begin to mount. Incorporate your daughter's therapy into your lifestyle so completely that it becomes part of what it means to grow up, and you're virtually certain to play a big role in making the therapy successful. Let me give you a fun example.

A while back, I treated a boy who would not take naps at preschool. His teachers were exasperated, because all the other kids in his class dutifully laid down on their little cots for an hour each afternoon. But not only would this little guy refuse to nap, he would scream bloody murder at the very idea of getting on his cot. He would disrupt the whole class, of course, and even if he eventually fell asleep for a few minutes, he invariably awakened before the others and would create a ruckus, making the situation untenable for everyone—him, his classmates, and, perhaps most of all, his teachers.

No one knew how to solve the problem. His parents reported that he napped quite happily and without incident at home, but they wanted him to succeed at school and hated the idea that he would have to be pulled out of the class. The teachers had begun to suspect the only solution would be for him to leave, but—as excellent advocates for their son—the parents were determined to try something else, first.

They approached us and asked us to observe their son in his classroom, which we did, in addition to interviewing them about his sleeping and napping habits at home. Following the site visit and consultation, we discovered that the cot was somewhat stiff, and that his blanket was very light. The cot was also positioned adjacent to a door that added noise and distraction from a hallway.

So, we recommended moving his cot to a quiet nook, and suggested the use of a weighted blanket. We placed a beanbag chair by the cot, so that when he awakened he could climb into the chair and look at his favorite books until the rest of the class was ready to wake. These few small changes made all the difference. The weighted blanket and bean bag chair offered him the proprioceptive input he needed to feel safe and comforted, while the repositioned cot led to less external distraction. After only a couple of days, he was able to transition to his nap without stress, returning the class and the teachers to the calm they all were seeking. His teachers were elated, and his parents were justifiably proud of their decision to get a bit of help in solving the problem creatively.

When It's Time to Stop

During the initial evaluation that precedes the start of therapy, therapists and parents jointly create a summary of the specific goals they intend to meet—objectives that are based on the parents' concerns and what the therapist has observed during the evaluation. These goals are typically based on what the combined major concerns are, what improvement everyone would like to see, and a desire to close any developmental gaps that are present. As time goes by in therapy, the child gets older, so the rate of progress needs to be faster than the actual chronological age, which means that—in addition to reaching the goals which were initially identified—we're also working on solidifying the child's sensory motor foundation, so the child will be able to continue to keep up on his own. In six months' time, we want to see more than a six-month developmental gain—we want to see eight, ten, or even fifteen months' worth of developmental gain. As long as a child is making progress in therapy and closing that gap, continued therapy is recommended.

When a child reaches the point when she no longer has an identifiable developmental delay, and her abilities and behaviors match those of the majority of her peers, we can wean her off of therapy onto a home program geared to support and continue this process at a normal rate. At this point, when children are happy and successful in their daily lives, when they don't have to struggle, and when parents clearly see and appreciate the changes, it is time for them to graduate to a home program.

A home program involving a consistent "sensory diet" must be maintained after therapy ends. It helps hold the progress that's been made and allows the child to continue to grow on the timetable he was intended. Without these continued activities, it is easy to slip back into old patterns and new problems can occur. The sensory diets most therapists recommend consist of exercises, activities, and experiences that they know from experience will keep a child on track and help ensure that he doesn't fall behind again and need to return for more therapy. Each sensory diet is tailored to the individual child and recommendations range from a martial arts class (in which kids continue to develop good bilateral coordination) to swimming programs and gymnastics.

Team sports like soccer and baseball also help to build social skills, while contributing to the ongoing development of the musculoskeletal system. I'm a fan of team sports—assuming that the kids are on track and can feel successful within the group. It's important to know your child and what their athletic preferences are, however. Other activities like martial arts, swimming, and even fencing (with face guards and swords) are great for kids as they transition out of therapy. These activities all do a great job of building coordination, body control, and attention. Physical exercise is vital for all of us throughout our lives, and as much exercise as possible is wonderful for kids as they leave therapy.

Children who have coordination problems tend to not develop a love of sports, at least not until they experience some success with their bodies. Their lack of coordination leads to inactivity, lack of interest, and a kind of vicious circle, because sports and exercise are actually the best ways to improve coordination, as well as focus and attention. Like adults, kids who don't exercise tend to have trouble organizing, completing activities, and staying focused. So, to maintain a child's new-found coordination and self-confidence when therapy is completed, it's critical to keep up with sports and exercise programs that can become an integral part of her life.

Give your child a voice in choosing the kinds of activities in which she is involved. Nothing's worse than insisting that your daughter takes twice-weekly karate lessons if she *hates* karate. Even though that may be a great activity to support her bilateral coordination, if she doesn't like it, it won't be helpful. By the same token, don't let your child's occasional frustration with a sport or other form of exercise lead to her refusal to participate in it. This can set her up to be a "quitter," which isn't a good thing either for therapy or for self-esteem. But, if you force a child into an activity that she really doesn't like or that is beyond her capabilities or comfort zone, the lesson she will learn is to avoid challenges of all kinds. Instead, set your child up for success by finding that "just-right" activity that allows her to have fun as she meets the challenge and succeeds at it, building up her self-esteem.

In addition to organized sports and exercise programs, there are also great activities you can encourage kids to do at home—from the simplicity of playing cards (which is excellent for building manual dexterity) to jumping on a trampoline (which offers great proprioceptive input and a quick way to get sensory needs met—I'm not sure what I would have done if we hadn't had a trampoline for our sons so that they could burn off excess energy). If you have a pool, build obstacle courses out of rubber mats the child can crawl across on the water, or have a balancing competition to see who can balance best on his knees on a kick-board. Be creative—and ask your child's therapists for suggestions.

Remember, too, that kids want and need quality time *with you* more than anything else. As often as you can, arrange activities that not only support their sensory diet, but also involve time with *you*. Build your emotional bonds and nurture the relationships that all kids need so that they can feel safe and secure in the world, as well as continuing to support the development of their brains and bodies.

Return for Tune-Ups

I remember a wonderful boy whose mother was a teacher and parent who really understood the meaning of continuing education. James was an uncoordinated child with weak posture, but he really flourished in therapy. He reached all of the milestones we set for him in record time, which resulted in improved school performance and healthy self-confidence. But he was going through a rapid phase of growth, gaining two inches in height in just a few months. Just like a puppy who needs to grow into its feet, he struggled to keep up with his motor skills as he grew. Whenever he went into one of these growth spurts, he would have a setback and his mother would bring him back in for a "tune-up." In ten or twelve weeks, he would be back to a place in which he was really flying again, and off he would go once more. Then, a year later, he would be back for another tune-up. We continued this relationship with James and his mother for many years, stopping when he reached sixteen. His dramatic growth spurts had slowed, and he had become a delightful young man whose life was filled with great promise.

I'm not suggesting that *every* child needs to return to therapy periodically. But some youngsters, like James, benefit greatly from this option. As your child continues to grow and develop, new issues sometimes arise, particularly if he still exhibits some developmental gaps. If you suspect your child could use a therapy tune-up, your instinct is likely correct. If you have questions, take your child to a therapist who knows him well by now, and discuss your concerns so you know what your options are.

When Your Child Stumbles

Keep in mind, too, that it's not uncommon for all kids to go through rough patches, even after their therapy goals have been met and they've begun to fly. Your child may well grow frustrated for a week or a month prior to making another big developmental jump—just like infants who are often very fussy as they begin to try to pull themselves up to stand or to walk.

About ten percent of the kids we treat have occasional setbacks that are significant enough that we hear about them in calls from concerned parents. During these times, CranioSacral Therapy can be helpful in calming down the child's autonomic nervous system and smoothing over some of the rough spots. Talking to a CranioSacral therapist who also does sensory integration therapy is ideal in this situation, as the therapist can help discern what's going on and make any suggestions for ways to help.

It is also not uncommon for kids to have a setback months—or even years—after leaving therapy. As they get older, they encounter new challenges of every kind. Simply because earlier goals have been met with the help of therapy, especially if underlying sensory motor needs have not been getting fully met for one reason or another, it doesn't guarantee that the road will remain smooth forever. Life just doesn't work like that, does it?

I always remind parents that you have to feed your garden with water and fertilizer in order to watch it grow and look as beautiful as it can. If you stop feeding it, it will wither. Something similar holds true for kids who have had sensory challenges. As they mature, if they no longer receive the kinds of physical activity and emotional connections that once helped them soar, new problems are likely to arise. Yet, there is never a reason to panic when you see a setback. Instead, be proactive and take stock of everything at play in your child's life, with a particular focus on her physical activity. Is she really engaging her body on a regular basis? Is she playing sports or exercising in ways that support coordination, bilateral movement, eye-hand interaction, and self-confidence? If not, explore new activities that sound exciting to her. Remind her that it's perfectly normal to be nervous as she begins new undertakings. Cheer her on as she challenges herself anew.

Once you know how to walk, you never have to relearn how, and the same holds true with all the tools that kids learn and acquire in therapy. They don't lose them, yet as they mature they must continue to acquire *new* skills. And if there is something getting in the way of acquiring them, then gaps can emerge again.

Puberty is a time in life when problems tend to re-surface. As kids' bodies begin to go through dramatic hormonal changes, new stresses of many kinds emerge. Body image becomes a real concern for the first time; relationships with parents, siblings, and friends can get complicated; kids often have to switch to new schools during those years, and the thrill and terror of romance begin to enter their lives.

Adolescence, in contrast to puberty, is the *psychological* time in which kids begin to try to make sense of who they truly are and what's most important to them. Peer pressure can become intense, and with it comes the risk of falling into the world of drugs and alcohol. Kids who have never found success, and who suffer from low self-esteem, tend to self-medicate more than others, using drugs or alcohol to numb a constant sense of inadequacy. Teenagers develop vital bonds with their friends and peer groups—and that can be very enriching—but when the group's focus is behavior that's dangerous, things can very quickly spiral out of control.

Maybe you remember your own adolescent years—perhaps not so fondly—so be sensitive to your child's ups and downs and know that professionals can help if they are needed, whether that means revisiting sensory-motor therapy, talking with a counselor, or simply taking another inventory of your child's sensory diet.

If your growing child seems less confident in his physical abilities, is having trouble concentrating, or isn't keeping up with his classmates, it may well be a sign that he's in the midst of a setback. Don't worry excessively about this, but don't ignore what you're witnessing either. Pay quiet attention and assess what might be helpful. Does more therapy appear to be the best option? Should you suggest new physical activities that will engage him, or return to activities that once proved to be both fun and beneficial, but that he's given up?

If you opt to take your child back to a clinic you used in the past because of your concerns, therapists there are likely to do a brief re-evaluation that will demonstrate whether she has kept up with her developmental progress. Let's imagine that she left therapy at age six, for example, after meeting her goals and reaching age-equivalent developmental levels. If the re-evaluation shows that she is developmentally age-equivalent now that she's nine, that tells us that she's continuing to build her motor skills and that something else is likely the issue. But, if the re-evaluation shows that she's at a seven-year-old developmental level, then something has gotten in the way and she has not continued to progress on her own.

That's a strong signal that something is still a bit awry in her nervous system and is inhibiting normal, healthy, and typical progression. She made excellent strides in the past, and she will make great progress again. A new round of therapy, or an extensively revised sensory diet, is probably what's called for.

Give Your Child Wings!

One of the greatest gifts we can give our children is a strong and enduring understanding of their value in the world and the self-confidence to know that they can meet and overcome any challenge that life presents. I believe that one of the true silver linings in any child's struggles with sensory integration issues is that by approaching them head on, she will inevitably learn how very capable she is of changing, growing, and becoming. During therapy, and in the years beyond, she'll prove to herself that she can always find ways to do things better, and she'll know the joy and pride that come with those accomplishments. That's truly enormous. Whether you have a bucketful of challenges or you're the most talented person in the world, if you don't feel great about who you are and what you're made of, what good is anything else?

No matter what age your child is now, one thing is certain: he will be an adult one day. He'll increasingly become his own decision maker, and, almost certainly, life will present hurdles that he'll have to surmount on his own. It's vital therefore for you to give your children the tools that will allow them to help them shape the best lives they can for themselves. Rather than solving their problems for them as they begin to mature, teach them self-reflection and decision-making skills, instead. Help them understand that the best lives are lived with intention and goals that are worth setting.

And, finally, please remember this: in three decades of working with children, I have *never* encountered a single child who did not do better, who did not improve, or who did not have a brighter future when we parted than when we met. Some kids thrive almost immediately. Others take more time, and a few need many years, yet they all find more success and joy in their progress than they would have otherwise had, no matter how far behind they were when they started.

All that's really required is for everyone to work together—on the same team at the same time—with each of us cognizant of the truth that kids don't come into the world to misbehave or to do things the hard way. Children are born wired for accomplishment, for challenge and success, and for fulfillment. It's our joy and duty to be the best examples and best guides we can be as our children grow and develop, so that each one of them can fly exactly as far as they have the potential to go.

CHAPTER 7

———•———

Alex out in the world
Things really can turn out great!

W hen Alex was about five years old, I remember, one day, I decided to re-arrange the furniture in our family room—and you can imagine my shock when the new arrangement absolutely freaked him out. He broke into tears in protest, wanting the room back the way it was—he was *not* happy, as transitions of any kind had never been his friend. Yet, in that instance, instead of complaining about the changes for a day or so, he continued to protest them for *weeks*. Things had been building for him over the past year, following the birth of his younger brother, and while he had embraced Max with loving arms, the furniture re-arrangement seemed to be his tipping point.

It was a reminder, too—as if I had needed one—that my first son could be a challenge. He was highly intelligent, quite active, often impulsive and temperamental, and it was virtually certain that if his father or I wanted him to do something, he would have a different idea. My background in child development and sensory integration made it all the more obvious to me that this kind of work would likely be a big help to him. When I opened my clinic, it was with Alex in mind and we all were happier for it—his teachers, his parents, and even Alex himself.

Alex's Passions

Alex was not the most athletic boy those first five years, yet he loved running around on the soccer field, typically doing his own thing rather than getting deeply involved in the game—something that's not unusual for a five year old. As he got a little older, we began to look for more opportunities for him to engage in physical activities with which he could build on his bilateral coordination and postural strength.

Somehow, we discovered fencing and Alex loved it from the start. He would put on his heavy fencing jacket and helmet and his entire persona would change. I probably shouldn't have been surprised. As a sensory development specialist, I knew proprioception was a great way to organize a body. Children who have a hard time sitting still and paying attention can often be helped with jumping breaks and lap pads that give them added proprioceptive input. It made perfect sense that, for Alex, wearing a heavy fencing jacket and knickers, gloves, and a stiff, wire-mesh face guard that enclosed his whole head felt *good* to him—to him it was enveloping and secure, rather than hot or claustrophobia-inducing (as some other kids might have felt). He thrived on the focus and concentration the sport demanded, as well as the one-on-one challenge it posed. It was like physical chess, and he loved it.

Alex's father grew up hunting, yet I hated guns and everything to do with them, so I'd never been thrilled by my son's fascination with toy soldiers and the elaborate war games he would create with them. It was a world I couldn't enter with him, yet I knew he was simply one of millions of boys who are drawn to this kind of play. Fencing, happily, was a way he was able to engage in a "physically appropriate" kind of combat that I could both understand and condone. I could readily see its many benefits for him—and I've recommended fencing (along with various martial arts) to hundreds of patients' parents ever since.

During Alex's first years of fencing, we took a family trip to the Cayman Islands, where we were staying at a lovely hotel. Alex was fascinated by an imposing safe located behind the reception desk that had big, impressive buttons, bolts, and a giant handle. He wanted to see how it opened. That didn't surprise me at all, but I was surprised when the hotel manager, who was working nearby, overhead Alex's request and jokingly invited him to come behind the counter and see the safe close at hand. In fact, the manager said that if Alex could open the safe, he would offer us a couple nights of free lodging.

Alex was thrilled. Not understanding that the manager was joking, he simply marched up to the safe and started pushing buttons and spinning dials, and—to everyone's astonishment—he then opened the safe's thick, heavy door. The manager was flabbergasted—then quickly concerned. He ordered the desk clerk to have the lock on the safe changed immediately, fearful that the hotel had something of a security problem. After all, if a six and a half year old could open a safe like that, who else could? The manager kept his word, though, offering us a complimentary stay, much to our delight.

That was a moment in which Alex was quintessentially his unique self—*very* observant, drawn to visual stimulation of every kind, and obsessive about those things that attracted him and the problems he loved to try to solve. I suspect that his keen eye had registered the combination when the clerk had opened the safe for another customer, and his ability to reproduce the action was my first real clue that he could memorize things almost instantly.

As Alex grew older and digital gaming technology evolved, *of course* he became fascinated by video games and the visual stimulation they provided. I would watch and be amazed by how immersed he would become in the game he was playing, by the rush that seemed to consume him, and I became concerned that there was an addictive quality to what this kind of visual stimulation provided him. After all, today, we know video games can be addictive, but twenty years ago this new technology was just being introduced. If I had known then what I know now, I would have done everything I could to keep him away from the mesmerizing video screens—or at least I would have limited the time he spent with them.

Off to School

When Alex was sixteen, it was my fear about the potential for another kind of addiction that prompted me to make changes in our lives. His father and I had recently divorced and Alex had taken the stress, complex emotions, and physical disruptions in our lives very hard. The experience was extremely difficult for him, as anyone might expect, and I hated seeing how our divorce and its aftermath seemed to be countering all the great gains he had made in his earlier years. We sought out family counseling to help all of us develop appropriate coping skills and resilience.

Max, four years Alex's junior, had always been easygoing, and although he was understandably sad about the divorce, he seemed to bounce back quickly and carry on without significant disruption in his life. But, for a boy like Alex—for whom even re-arranged furniture had proven capable of causing him stress when he was younger—the divorce was overwhelming. Many children with sensory processing challenges approach life rather "rigidly," seeking structure and organization everywhere they can find it. Alex was one of them, and not only did he have to deal with his family life turning upside down, he also had just entered high school, which was a brand new experience in virtually every way—with steadily increasing hormones added into the mix.

Alex often seemed to simply "check out" as a way to deal with his challenges. He lost interest in a number of activities he previously had been passionate about; during his sophmore year his teachers reported regression and a lack of effort on his part; and he made it plain that he had *no* interest whatsoever in studying or in extra-curricular activities at school. It was a significant concern to me that, while he was in an excellent private school, it was also a school in which student use of drugs and alcohol appeared to be an increasing problem. I could readily envision that he was at risk for going down that difficult road, given his background and the current challenges in his life.

After much debate, I made the decision to send him halfway across the country to a renowned prep school in Virginia—one with highly structured academics and student life and an engaged and supportive faculty. It was one of those rare times when, as a parent—and even though it was one of the hardest decision of my life—I felt as though I was absolutely doing the right thing. There really were no other choices in Dallas at that time, and I knew he needed to find some uninterrupted success somewhere.

To my delight, Alex thrived in Virginia. His junior year was a great success, and he had many new friends. His first report card included straight As; he joined the wrestling team, thrived as a wrestler, and developed a great mentoring relationship with his coach. He fell in love for the first time with a girl from a neighboring prep school, and I was thrilled to see what a great turn his young life was taking.

But, when Alex returned to Virginia to begin his senior year, three blows hit him immediately. He discovered that the wrestling coach who had become such an important mentor for him would not be back; his girlfriend informed him that she was ending their relationship, and— back home—his dog died. He quickly became depressed, as many kids would have done in a similar situation, but he took it harder than most. Rather than simply let him work things out on his own far away from home, it seemed like the better option would be to bring him back home where he could finish high school at a nearby alternative high school. And, happily, with close family support and some "tune-up" counseling, he began to thrive again.

Alex's Life

Alex completed his senior year with straight As once again, although it seemed clear that he was turned off to school at that point and was not interested in going straight into college. I should have anticipated that this lifelong contrarian of mine would do the one thing I feared most—that he would choose to go into the military—but little did I know that this was something he actually really wanted to do. Did he *really* want to be a soldier? I repeatedly asked him.

He thought he might, he said, and—in perfect Alex style—he threw himself into his research. He would have loved to learn to fly jets for the air force, but he knew his poor vision would make that impossible. So, he spoke extensively with navy, marine, and army recruiters. He took exams and scored so highly that West Point contacted him with an offer, but school was not what he wanted. He wanted "action" and to "see the world", he said. He ultimately settled on the army, and—despite my fears—I knew that this was Alex's life and he had reached the age at which he needed to be making his own decisions.

As a therapist, there was a part of me that was able to understand why the army appealed to him so much and why it might be a great fit for him. A highly structured environment with plenty of rules had increasingly proved to be an environment in which he thrived. He had been fascinated by war games and soldiering since he was a little boy; he'd proven in fencing that "fighting" of a certain kind was a challenge that he was drawn to; he loved the tactics and strategies of video games—and what could be better for his proprioceptive system than long days spent drilling in heavy boots, helmets, and flak jackets, while shouldering an eighty-pound pack?

A few months later, Alex reported from basic training to tell me how happy he was about the decision he had made. He was thriving. In his first year as a soldier he was selected to learn Arabic after scoring high on his defensive language aptitude battery test and then, sure enough, he was off to Iraq for a year. During his tour, his ears were damaged by noise exposure, but otherwise he wasn't injured. He decided to re-enlist, transferring out of the infantry to become a combat medic, then, while training in Fort Sam Houston in San Antonio, he was accepted into the army's prestigious Civil Affairs unit.

Imagine my mix of emotions. I still worried about his safety, but I was immensely proud, too, that he had understood what was right for him and what kinds of life experiences he wanted to have following high school. I was even happier when he made the choice to become a medical practitioner and would soon discover something of that role's challenges and its many rewards.

Alex is out of the army now, although he continues to serve our country in the National Guard. He's a proud veteran, and I am enormously proud of him, while he prepares for his next life adventures. He is back in school, serious about business and civil affairs. For awhile I thought he might want to go into physical therapy—just like his mom did a very long time ago—but for now I'm delighted that he is able to share his gift of working with children by working part time in our therapy clinics.

It's wonderful to have him with us as a tech, participating as a vital part of our team. As the only male on the staff—and as a young man full of enthusiasm and charisma—all the kids who come to the clinic think he's an absolute rock star. He's an incredible motivator for them—and can *really* relate to them, it goes without saying—and he works closely with the therapists, who appreciate his insights and his dedication. Honestly, I don't think I've ever seen him happier than he is when he's in the gym working with a child who has challenges similar to those that have shaped his own life.

Alex, like each of the rest of us, will always have to confront tests and trials. He will be expected to bring his own unique set of gifts and limitations to the task of making the most of his life. I'm happy to say that, with him working alongside me these days, I can't help but feel that things have come full circle in the two decades since I created a clinic specifically to get him the developmental help he needed.

In the end, I believe the foremost thing that therapy gave him was a kind of resilience he otherwise might not have, and, in my experience, resiliency is one of the most vital "life tools" that each of us can possess—the ability to creatively work through whatever situations arise, to pick ourselves back up when we stumble, and to renew our hopes time after time after time.

An Afterword

———•———

A lex is an adult now, and my job of raising him is complete. When I offer him advice these days, it's much more often about how he can better assist children with sensory challenges at the clinic than it is about issues personal to him. And what I try to communicate with Alex—who will be a parent himself someday—I also can share with those of you who have read this book because of your desire to help your own children overcome sensory challenges.

Professional therapists have precisely the same goals when working with your child as you do. We want your child to have the very best life possible. Nothing is more important than your child, and we understand that. Yet, in working with children to help make them more coordinated, less fearful, more focused, better readers and writers, and more adept at the their interactions with others, we are always moving toward two larger and more important goals.

The first of those primary goals is to give all children some of that resiliency I just spoke of—the ability to successfully surmount whatever issues come their way. When we are able to help instill that ability in them beginning when they are four or five or six years old, we help them help themselves as they continue to develop and mature. By the time a child grows up and becomes independent, if they have learned how to recover creatively from whatever life throws at them, then we've done our jobs well—both as therapists and as parents.

The second overarching goal—and perhaps the most important of all for veteran therapists like me, nascent therapists like Alex, and every parent of every child—is to do everything we possibly can to help the kids in our care *feel good about who they are*, and then to give them the tools to be independent and successful in all aspects of their lives. It's a simple goal, but it's profoundly important. It's the bedrock on which every well-lived life is built.

I've been deeply blessed both as a mother and as a developmental specialist to have spent so much of my life helping kids develop real resiliency, self-confidence, and self-love. (What richer life than that could anyone have?) And, as a parent, that same blessing has been given to you as well, and I wish you enormous good luck as you take that gift and responsibility both seriously and joyfully.

There's no better job in the world than helping your child see how very far he can fly!

QUESTIONS PARENTS OFTEN ASK

——•——

How early can a sensory challenge be detected?

Different symptoms occur at different times of development. A baby may show symptoms of irritability, sleep disturbances, or lack of attachment. A toddler may have trouble transitioning (going from one environment or activity to another without a negative change in behavior), potty training, or interacting with others. A school-age child may have difficulty learning, struggle with peers, have poor handwriting, or show increasing signs of anxiety. There is no need to look for trouble, but be aware if your child is having more trouble than others—and be proactive. There is no harm in seeking out an evaluation. If you discover something early, consider it a gift and jump on it. You will be able to make greater gains over shorter periods of time. If you discover something later on, know that it can be treated, but may take more time.

My baby was born with a physical birth defect. Will this affect her sensory motor development?

Just because your child has a physical challenge does not mean she will have sensory motor challenges as well. However, it can make things more challenging to get her sensory-motor needs met. Do whatever you can to provide meaningful vestibular, proprioceptive, and tactile sensory experiences to set your child up for success.

Once my child starts therapy, how many sessions will it take before we start seeing some improvement?

It typically takes approximately six months for actual neurologic change to occur. This does not mean that you won't see progress before then. Think of the changes a baby makes between birth and six months. He goes from being an utterly dependent newborn to an infant starting to crawl, but this doesn't happen overnight. The same happens when you start to give the nervous system new physical input through sensory integration therapy. Your child may want to try new things for the first time, or may simply feel generally better about himself. You may not see change right away, but this is setting the stage for bigger milestones. Don't look for anything specific, but embrace her successes and you'll be surprised at what happens relatively quickly.

What can I do at home to help speed up the process?

Understanding what your child's underlying sensory motor needs are can help set your child up for maximal success. A lot can be said for anticipating sensory motor needs before your child becomes over-stimulated, or having the appropriate activities at hand to get your child into the "just right" arousal level, setting her up for optimal learning and interactions. A "sensory diet" of activities to do at home is also an important part of your child's progress. These can help provide you and your child with activities geared toward building new optimal neural pathways. Once you are in therapy, talk to your child's therapist about what his "sensory diet" should be.

If my oldest child has sensory differences, will my other children have them as well?

Not necessarily. And, if they do have sensory challenges, each one will likely present them differently. All children are different; even identical twins are different in how they interpret their sensory worlds. Treat each one of your children as individuals, and you'll be on the right track.

What is a "sensory tune-up"?

After your child is discharged from therapy, you may want to think about checking in every six months to two years. If progress is slowing down, or your child is experiencing an increasing number of challenges again, a sensory tune-up may be just the thing to jumpstart him back into gear. It is typically a shorter run of therapy (one to three months) aimed at getting him back on track. Remember: as a child gets older, things tend to become more of a challenge. If he is having trouble keeping up without intervention, it's good to periodically re-address the situation.

Is my child better off going to a public or private school?

This decision is up to you—and will require some research. Visit different schools to see what kinds of programs they offer and ask questions: How big are their classes? How do they address learning differences? Does their staff receive frequent in-service training, and are they vested in helping kids be successful in loving to learn? If your child is in therapy, you might ask your therapists for suggestions of what to look for in a classroom for your child—and then be sure to ask the school whether that can be provided.

How should I talk to my friends and family about my child's developmental challenges? What should I do if they refuse to believe it, or dismiss it as a phase?

Believe in your child. Be realistic and honest, and be your child's advocate. Remember, you want to set him up for success! People tend to make their own labels or explanations for behaviors they see. You are your daughter's parent and know her better than anyone else. You know what's right for your child. Stick to your guns!

What do you think about special programs and supplements I see advertised that claim to produce dramatic results in a short period of time?

Remember, there is no "quick fix" for anything developmental! Even normal development takes time. Understand what your child's needs are and be consistent in your efforts to support those needs, and the changes will come. Your goal should be to maximize your child's actual potential. Embrace the journey, and things will get better! You can't change anyone except yourself, but you can help set the stage to get the maximum results for your child.

How do children with sensory issues benefit from CranioSacral Therapy?

CranioSacral Therapy is a great way to promote ideal functioning of the central nervous system, by allowing the body to relax deeply and release tight muscle and tissue restriction. When this occurs, everything works better. Because there are no medications involved, and it is not invasive, this treatment has no down side and is always worth a try. Children who receive CST in conjunction with other treatments seem to go further and faster in their other treatments.

I'm totally overwhelmed with my child's challenges. What can I do to reduce my own stress level and get a grip on the situation?

Join a support group. Get a massage or a CST treatment of your own.

Exercise! Educate yourself on what is going on with your child and understand that we are all works in progress. Licensed professional counselors can also be a tremendous help in developing strategies to reduce your stress and process your feelings effectively. Do not be afraid to seek out counseling for yourself; it can be a godsend for everyone involved.

Is there something I can do to improve my child's handwriting skills?
There is always more to handwriting than meets the eye. Very often, messy writing is caused by poor bilateral coordination or challenged visual motor skills. Handwriting is dependent on adequate eye-hand coordination, muscle control, and postural stability. By encouraging your child to participate in activities that support these areas, you can indirectly help improve your child's handwriting. Activities like martial arts, swimming, and gymnastics are all great integrating activities that indirectly support handwriting.

What's the difference between early intervention programs, therapy at school, and therapy at a clinic?
All are good, but each is very different from the others. Early intervention programs focus on the family and provide input to help your child *at home* utilizing techniques that family members can employ. School-based therapy focuses on educational goals. Typically, children who receive therapy in schools get about twenty minutes of intervention once or twice a week for services that focus on educational goals, such as how to hold a pencil or how to better organize work. Private physical and/or occupational therapy addresses the underlying causes of a challenge and focuses on the root of the problem, not the symptom. Sessions are frequently scheduled for one hour, twice a week.

How can I tell if my child has ADHD or Sensory Integration challenges—and is there a difference in the treatment?

The symptoms of both ADHD and sensory integration disorder can include hyperactivity, inattention, and impulsivity, among other things. Sorting out these two conditions can be difficult—even for professionals—but it is much easier to figure out the right kind of therapy to start with. Drugs don't create new neural pathways—sensory integration therapy does. Before considering starting with medication in a young, developing nervous system, an attempt should be made to do whatever you can to set your child up for interacting with the physical cues around him more appropriately, first. This is what sensory integration therapy does. Even if your child has been diagnosed with ADHD by a physician, sensory integration therapy can help him to become more organized and attentive in his environment, especially before he hits adolescence. It also provides him with an opportunity to develop his nervous system to work better for him, lessening the chance that he may have to be on medication for this in the future. For older children (and on through adulthood), other therapies like the Interactive Metronome and counseling can be additionally helpful in treating symptoms of inattention and impulsivity, lessening the need for medication, as well.

How long are most kids in therapy?

The typical length of therapy for mild to moderate sensory integration problems is one to two years. Remember, there is no quick fix, but we can certainly help! The sooner we start, the quicker you'll see changes. I have never seen a child who did not improve with sensory motor therapy. I see the greatest benefits when parents are consistent over a long period of time. This helps to solidify the child's foundation, paving the way for greater success over time.

GLOSSARY

---•---

ADD/ADHD: Attention deficit disorder (ADD) and attention deficit hyperactivity disorder (ADHD) are medical conditions characterized by a child's inability to focus, while possessing impulsivity, fidgeting, and inattention. Both conditions can adversely affect a child's educational performance.

Asymmetrical Tonic Neck Reflex: A primitive reflex that is present from birth but should disappear by six months of age. If an infant is lying on its back and the head is turned to one side, the arm and leg on the side to which the head is turned should straighten, and the arm and leg on the opposite side should bend (this is referred to as the "fencer" position). The continued presence of these primitive reflexes after six months may indicate a developmental delay associated with poor balance, poor bilateral coordination, no hand dominance (being neither right- or left-handed), poor handwriting, and limited written expression.

Autism: A developmental disability affecting verbal and nonverbal communication, as well as social interaction, which is generally evident before age three. Autism frequently adversely affects a child's social and educational performance. Other characteristics often associated with autism are: engaging in repetitive activities and movements, resistance to environmental change or change in daily routines, and unusual responses to sensory experiences.

Bilateral Coordination: The ability to use both sides of the body at the same time in a controlled and organized manner. Having efficient bilateral coordination enables both feet and/or both hands to work together, allowing fluid body movements and supporting the development of fine-motor skills, the ability to use tools, and the ability to visually track a moving object.

Bone Conduction: The transmission of sound to the inner ear through the bones of the skull. Bone conduction can be used to relay sound to individuals with normal or impaired hearing. Various listening programs utilize bone conduction. This is also how babies who are in utero perceive sound before they are born.

Centers for Disease Control and Prevention (CDC): The U.S. national public health institute that conducts and supports health promotion, as well as disease prevention and preparedness activities in the United States, with the goal of improving overall public health.

Cerebellum: The area of the brain that controls motor movement coordination, balance, equilibrium, and muscle tone.

Child Advocacy: The act of assisting, defending, and protecting a child's interests and rights. Child advocates may be parents, family members, guardians, teachers, and/or professionals who seek to speak out on behalf of a child's best interest. Child advocates may work on an individual, group, or governmental level to help protect and nurture children. As parents, we all have the responsibility to advocate on behalf of our children for their greatest good.

Child Find: A government-mandated program that identifies, locates, and evaluates individuals with disabilities from birth to twenty-one years of age. Child Find is available through all public school systems in the United States.

Cognitive Ability: The process in the brain used for thinking, remembering, reasoning, understanding, and making decisions.

Colic: A condition which is defined as episodes of crying for more than three hours a day for more than three days a week—and for three consecutive weeks—in an otherwise well-fed, healthy child between the age of two weeks and four months.

Container Babies: A slang term for a baby that spends a majority of her time in car seats, infant swings, vibrating chairs, and other devices that expose the infant to very limited actual movement experiences.

Core Musculature: Muscles in the body's lower and upper torso that are important to maintaining proper posture, as well as protecting the inner organs. Building core musculature is essential for staying strong and balanced, and for allowing children to sit still in order to develop fine-motor skills like handwriting.

CranioSacral Therapists: Trained professionals who identify and treat imbalances within the CranioSacral system. A CranioSacral therapist works to relieve pain and dysfunction as well as enhance overall body performance and whole-body health. Anyone with a "license to touch" can learn how to become a CranioSacral therapist. Professionals who might utilize this skill include physical therapists, occupational therapists, massage therapists, nurses, doctors, dentists, speech therapists, and chiropractors, etc.

CranioSacral Therapy (CST): A non-invasive, hands-on therapeutic technique used to relieve pain, tension, and body dysfunction, while improving whole-body health and performance. CST has been found to enhance sensory function, motor coordination, developmental progress, neuromuscular function, and overall health. Developed by Dr. John E. Upledger, CST's effectiveness has been substantiated by more than forty years of research and clinical studies.

Developmental Delay: An expression that describes the condition of a child who is behind in at least one area of development in one or more of the following areas: physical development, cognitive development, communication, social or emotional development, or behavioral development.

Developmental Disabilities: A group of conditions defined by an impairment in the physical, cognitive, language, and/or behavior areas. These conditions impact day-to-day functioning, and may last throughout a person's lifetime. About one in six children in the U.S. have one or more developmental disabilities or other developmental delays, according to the Centers for Disease Control and Prevention.

Developmental Pediatrician: A medical doctor who has subspecialty training in developmental-behavioral pediatrics, and who can evaluate, counsel, and provide treatment for children and adolescents with a wide range of developmental and behavioral difficulties.

Disability: The consequence of an impairment that may be physical, cognitive, mental, sensory, emotional, and/or developmental, and which limits normal daily activities. Some people are born with a disability, while other disabilities occur as a result of an illness or injury, and some people develop them as they age. About one in every five people in the United States has a disability, according to the U.S. National Library of Medicine and the National Institutes of Health.

Dysgraphia: A learning disability that negatively affects the act of writing, which requires a complex set of motor and information processing skills. Dysgraphia can lead to problems with spelling, as well as difficulties organizing letters and numbers, and putting thoughts on paper (in essence impacting all written expression).

Early Childhood Intervention program (ECI): A federally mandated program that provides services to children from birth to three years who have disabilities and developmental delays. The Individuals with Disabilities Education Act (IDEA) requires that every state and territory of the United States provide early intervention services to eligible children and families.

Early Intervention: Therapeutic services that help infants and toddlers with disabilities or delays learn key skills and advance in their development. Research shows that 80% of a child's development occurs before she reaches the age of five. For this reason, it is critical that an infant or toddler who has been identified with a developmental delay or disability has an opportunity to receive early intervention therapy.

Eustachian Tubes: The tubes that connect the middle ears to the back of the throat, which help the ears drain fluid, as well as keeping air pressure in the ears at appropriate levels.

Fine-Motor Skills: The movement and control of small muscle groups that allow for refined movement patterns essential for tasks such as handwriting, drawing, playing a musical instrument, and many other activities.

Gait: The pattern of how a person walks. Different types of walking problems occur without a person's control and an unusual gait may signal an underlying disability or muscular or structural imbalance.

Gross-Motor Skills: The movement of large muscle groups necessary to perform activities such as running, jumping, and skipping.

Gustatory System: The sensory system that detects five specific tastes: salty, sweet, bitter, sour, and savory.

Hyperactivity: An apparent condition of constant movement. It is often associated with being easily distracted, impulsive, unable to concentrate, aggressive, or displaying other, similar behaviors.

Hypersensitivity: The result of being abnormally sensitive and reactive to an environment. Sound, sights, touch, smell, taste, and/or emotional stimuli can cause the body to react adversely. Hypersensitivity in one or more areas may indicate a sensory integration disorder.

Hypertonia: A condition in which there is too much muscle tone, impacting an individual's motor function and ability to stretch. Hypertonia can occur for many reasons, including birth trauma, a blow to the head, stroke, brain tumor, the influence of toxins that affect the brain, and/or neurodegenerative diseases.

Hypotonia: A condition in which low muscle tone causes laxity around the joints. This causes a joint to be hypermobile (also known as being "double jointed"). Usually detected at birth or during infancy, hypotonia can be caused by a variety of diseases and disorders. A person with hypotonia often needs more muscle strength than a person with normal tone, just to help normalize muscle function and protect the body from injury (like breaking a bone during a fall).

IDEA: The 1990 Individuals with Disabilities Education Act. IDEA is a federal law that ensures the availability of services for children with disabilities. It gives each state the authority to create its own program, yet each must to comply with federal IDEA requirements to receive funding.

Integrated Listening Systems (iLs): A patented multi-sensory program for improving brain function. ILs programs improve emotional regulation while training the brain to process sensory information. With improved regulation and processing, our ability to focus, think, and engage successfully in social situations also improves. It is used frequently to treat attention and coordination problems, as well as to enhance sports performance.

Interactive Metronome (IM): A research-based training program that improves a person's rhythm and timing, increasing the brain's ability to plan, sequence, and process information more effectively. IM promotes attention, coordination, sports performance, behavioral control, and core mental skills. (For more information, see: www.interactivemetronome.com.)

Learning Disabilities: Difficulties in learning due to how a person's brain processes information. Sensory integration dysfunction is often associated with learning differences. Children with learning disabilities can be as smart or smarter than their peers, but have trouble with attention, reading, writing, spelling, math, reasoning, recalling, and/or organizing information.

Midline: The theoretical line that runs down the body from head to toe, dividing the body into left and right "halves." "Crossing the midline" refers to the ability to move a part of the body—such as a hand or foot—into the space of the other hand or foot. Even the eyes have to cross the body's midline when they move independently from the head in order to look left and right. Being able to cross the midline indicates that a child has reached the point in his or her development that the right and left sides of the brain are working in tandem.

Milestones: A set of functional skills or age-specific tasks that most children can do within a certain age range. Pediatricians use milestones to help gauge how a child is developing. Developmental milestones can involve physical, social, emotional, cognitive, and/or communication skills such as walking, sharing with others, expressing emotions, recognizing familiar sounds, and talking. Failure to achieve a particular milestone by a given age range may indicate a developmental delay or a sensory processing challenge.

Motor Planning: The ability of children to imagine a mental strategy to carry out a movement or action. Motor planning involves a number of abilities, including the visual detection of motion and errors in movement, selection of responses, and self-corrective motions.

Musculoskeletal systems: The body's bones, muscles, cartilage, tendons, ligaments, joints, and other connective tissue that supports and binds tissues and organs together. Collectively, these body parts create the framework for the body, as well as its movements and degree of flexibility.

Normal Development: The acquisition of certain skills and abilities that follows a known and predictable course in the expected amount of time. Crawling, walking, saying single words, and following directions are examples of predictable achievements. Although not all children reach each milestone (see above) at the exact same age, there is an expected time frame for reaching each normal developmental marker.

Occupational Therapist: A medically degreed and licensed professional who is trained in the evaluation and treatment of patients with physical, cognitive, and/or emotional challenges. (See also "Physical Therapist.")

Occupational Therapy (OT): Therapy provided by a licensed occupational therapist aimed at increasing the physical function of motor skills, academic performance, handwriting, social skills, and sensory integration while promoting independence and healthy self-esteem. OT is used to treat a variety of health concerns, including: developmental disabilities, autism spectrum disorder, sensory integration deficits, developmental differences, cerebral palsy, genetic disorders, injuries due to accidents, sports injuries, and surgical rehabilitation. (See also "Physical Therapy.")

Oculomotor: Prefix relating to the eye and the sense of motor and visual perceptual skills.

Olfactory System: The sensory system that is related to the sense of smell.

Physical Therapist: A medically degreed and licensed professional who is trained to evaluate and treat disorders of the human body, primarily by physical means, to improve physical function and alleviate pain. (See also "Occupational Therapist.")

Physical Therapy (PT): Therapy provided by a licensed physical therapist aimed at improving motor development, strength, balance, coordination, gait, and self-confidence. PT is used to treat a wide range of health concerns, including: movement difficulties and related functional problems, sensory integration deficits, developmental disabilities, autism spectrum disorder, sports injuries, and surgical rehabilitation. (See also "Occupational Therapy.")

Picky Eater: A term used to describe a child who dislikes many foods and will only eat a limited number of foods. Although many people assume a picky eater chooses foods based on taste, choices of foods are often associated with a tactile aversion or hypersensitivity to touch or smell, or due to having a muscle imbalance in the mouth.

Plagiocephaly: A disorder in which the back, or one side, of an infant's head is flattened as the result of spending too much time lying on his back or being in a position where the head is resting against a flat surface for prolonged periods of time, such as in car seats, cribs, strollers, swings, or playpens.

Proprioception: The awareness of posture, movement, or changes in equilibrium, and the knowledge of position, weight, and resistance of objects in relation to the body. The proprioceptive system provides critical processing information through the body's joints, ligaments, and muscles.

Red Flag: A sign that there is a problem that demands attention and needs to be corrected.

Reflux: A condition where the contents of the stomach are spit out, usually shortly after feeding. Spitting up (infant reflux) becomes less common as a baby gets older.

Sensory Integration Disorder: A neurological condition in which external or internal sensory information gets "mixed up" in the brain and produces a response that is inappropriate to the context.

Sensory Integration Therapy: Therapeutic treatment that promotes normal growth and development by helping individuals improve their motor ability, strength, and overall physical function, while enhancing their learning skills, and quality of life. Sensory integration therapy treats children of all ages who have one or more difficulties with coordination, gross- and fine-motor skills, learning differences, social interactions, and over- or underdeveloped sensitivities to movement, touch, sound, sight, taste, and smell. Therapy is provided through activities that involve the vestibular, proprioceptive, and tactile systems.

Sensory System: Part of the nervous system responsible for processing sensory information. This includes visual (sight), auditory (hearing), tactile (touch), olfactory (smell), gustatory (taste), vestibular (balance), and proprioceptive (awareness of muscles and movement) sensory information.

Sudden Infant Death Syndrome (SIDS): The unexplained death, usually during sleep, of a seemingly healthy baby who is less than a year old. Most doctors believe that SIDS is caused by a number of factors,

However, the rates for SIDS has gone down dramatically since doctors began recommending that babies sleep on their backs rather than on their stomachs.

Tactile Defensiveness: A negative response or increased sensitivity to texture or touch.

Therapeutic Modality: Any of a variety of methods (modes) a physical or occupational therapist might use to treat a patient, depending on the situation being presented.

Tone (Muscle): The degree of tension normally present in the resting state of a muscle. A person with "high tone" (or "hypertonia") tends to be very stiff, whereas a person with "low tone" (or "hypotonia") tends to be very "loose" or, in extreme cases, "floppy."

Torticollis: Abnormal tilting or twisting of the head and neck. In newborns, torticollis can result from the baby's positioning in the womb or from a difficult childbirth. It can also be caused by static positioning after birth, as can plagiocephaly (see above).

Transitioning: This is a term that frequently applies to how a child moves (or "transitions") from one environment to the next. Children who have trouble with transitions often have negative changes in their behavior as a result. These could include hyperactivity, increased frustration, clinging behaviors, crying, and/or resistance to direction.

Unilateral: Affecting or occurring on only one side of the body.

Vestibular Stimulation: Stimulation of the vestibular apparatus (bones of the inner ear and ear canals) that provide information regarding acceleration and the position of the body in space. Used to improve balance, coordination, movement, and eye coordination.

ACKNOWLEDGMENTS

———•———

*W*hen *Kids Fly* is a book that's had a long gestation, and I'm sure it still would be struggling to enter the world without the help and encouragement of many people along the way. Mark, my wonderful husband and organizer, thank you for your constant enthusiasm for this project, propelling it to completion. Alex and Max, my two incredible sons, you have been my greatest teachers and continue to make me smile every day. My three fantastic step-children, Jonathan, Christina, and Jeffrey, your collective words of encouragement and support have also reinforced the depth and blessings that I feel children bring to our lives, even when they are grown.

I am also thankful for the extremely talented therapists at the Integrative Pediatric Therapy clinics who do an amazing job every day, helping children develop into happy, healthy, and capable individuals. I'm grateful for all you do for the children we see. You are an exceptional group of therapists and the children we care for are very lucky to have you in their lives.

To my wonderful office staff, thank you for your immeasurable support in helping me find the time to make this happen. LaRae Steadman and Jamie Felton, your encouragement and "behind the scenes" organization will forever be appreciated.

Thank you to Woody Buckner for spurring me on to make this a dream come true, Judy Katz for getting me started, Russell Martin for helping me develop a book I am now proud to share, and Robert Schmidt of Bascom Hill Publishing Group for helping me bring it into its final form.

And, finally, a deeply heartfelt salute to all the families and children whom I have had the privilege of serving throughout the years. My life has been enriched by each of you! *Thank you!*

Sally Fryer Dietz

ABOUT THE AUTHOR

———◆———

For the past thirty-four years, Sally Fryer Dietz's focus and passion in the field of physical therapy has been in working with children. Not only is she a developmental expert, child advocate, and leading authority in therapeutic pediatrics, but she is also the mother two great children, one of whom had signs of a learning difference when he was a child. She counts her own children as being her greatest teachers, who have provided her with insight and empathy into the challenges universal to all parents, especially when something doesn't seem "quite right" with a child.

The first ten years of her professional career were spent working in San Francisco, at California Pacific Medical Center. There, she developed a great foundation for working with a diverse population of adults and children in a hospital setting, and also had the opportunity to spend time in an outpatient sensory integration clinic. Little did she know at that time that working with children with conditions from mild to moderate learning differences to severe autism and combining physical therapy and sensory integration techniques would lead her to starting her own clinic with her son in mind, fifteen years later in Dallas, Texas. Over the years, certifications in Sensory Integration and Praxis Testing ("SIPT" certification), CranioSacral Therapy, Interactive Metronome (IM), and Integrated Listening System (iLs) all followed.

Recognizing the high incidence of multiple challenges for children with learning differences and developmental delays, in 1994, she developed one of the first physical therapy practices in Dallas that coordinated with other pediatric specialists under the same roof. This allowed parents (including herself) to not have to run all over town to get multiple services. In 1998, Integrative Pediatric Therapy (IPT) was incorporated to provide a comprehensive treatment facility which included physical, occupational, speech, and CranioSacral therapists working together to meet the needs of the children they served. Since it's founding, IPT has grown to include three clinics in the Dallas area, including one at the Shelton School, the largest private school for learning-challenged children in Texas.

Dietz attributes the success of the children they have treated to having therapists who have a true passion for working with children and families and never settling for the "status quo." She believes there are no limits when it comes to a child's potential. Her son, Alex, who was five when she started her practice, is now twenty-six. He became a medical specialist in the army and is currently pursuing a career in civil affairs. Her continued quest for higher knowledge and for how she can best serve her patients continues to this day as she continues to be dedicated to helping children, students, new therapists, and families.

INDEX

Page numbers in **bold** indicate glossary entries.